Whodunit -You Decide!

Mini-Mysteries for You to Solve

Hy Conrad

Illustrated by Lucy Corvino

Sterling Publishing Co., Inc.
New York

Edited by Jeanette Green

Library of Congress Cataloging-in-Publication Data

Conrad, Hy.
    Whodunit—you decide! : mini-mysteries for you to solve / Hy
Conrad : illustrated by Lucy Corvino.
        p.   cm.
    Includes index.
    ISBN 0-8069-6150-3
    1. Puzzles.   2. Detective and mystery stories.   I. Title.
GV1507.D4C68   1996
793.73—dc20   96-25416

12   14   16   18   20   19   17   15   13   11

Published by Sterling Publishing Co., Inc.
387 Park Avenue South, New York, NY 10016
© 1996 by Hy Conrad
Distributed in Canada by Sterling Publishing
^c/o Canadian Manda Group, 165 Dufferin Street
Toronto, Ontario, Canada M6K 3H6
Distributed in Great Britain and Europe by Chris Lloyd at Orca Book
Services, Stanley House, Fleets Lane, Poole BH15 3AJ, England
Distributed in Australia by Capricorn Link (Australia) Pty. Ltd.
P.O. Box 704, Windsor, NSW 2756, Australia

Sterling ISBN 0-8069-6150-3

Contents

Opening Statement

I love a twisty mistery—the locked room, the impossible crime, the pivotal piece of evidence that appears to make no sense even though it has to. I love it when the writer plays with my mind, but plays fair. I love to slowly turn the story inside out and finally discover that elegantly simple twist that once made the author laugh out loud and say, "They'll never untangle this one."

The traditional "whodunit" does not hinge on police techniques, trivia, or even pure logic. It is based on imagination, and I'm often disappointed at how few real whodunits are being written these days. Arthur Conan Doyle, Agatha Christie, and Ellery Queen, the masters of the genre, were always clever and never too annoyingly complex.

Whodunit—You Decide! is my attempt to revive a taste of this classic form. All twelve of these murder mysteries, unraveled in the courtroom, share the same premise. Someone stands accused of a crime. And it is up to the jury—you the readers—to untangle the evidence and to find the defendant guilty or not guilty. Of course, as you'll discover, it's never that simple. There's always a twist. Was the murder a frame-up? Was it an accident? Was a suicide made to look like murder? Or did something even more devious happen?

Begin by reading one of the court cases in this book. Consider the "Trial Witnesses & Evidence" section at the end of the story, and note the minimum number of clues required to reach an informed verdict. Choose from the five possibilities which piece(s) of evidence you'll review first. Examine the clues one at a time, and try to digest each clue before you consider the next.

Very few readers will be able to solve a case and reach a verdict in the recommended minimum number of clues. Most readers will need to wade through all five pieces of evidence before going into deliberation. In the "Jury Deliberations" section you, as a member of the sitting jury, must review the evidence and try to make sense of it. If your budding theory fails to address all the concerns debated in jury deliberations, then return to the account of the crime and the evidence. Take your time in reviewing the case, and try to tie up all loose ends before you finally look up the solution in the "Verdicts" section.

Classic whodunits rank among the purest forms of puzzle; they ask you to make delicious sense out of what's seemingly contradictory. So, please relax and enjoy them. Devising these devilish twisters demanded a lot of hair-pulling and laughing out loud. I hope you'll have just as much fun solving them as I did creating them.

Hy Conrad

Our Man in the Field

At 9:08 P.M., a silent alarm rang at Ajax Security Co., sending an armed guard to the midtown branch of First National Bank. When he arrived on the scene, the guard discovered masked men scooping $20 bills out of the automatic-teller machines. One of the burglars physically attacked the guard, getting his own mask torn off in the fight and revealing his face to the bank's video system.

Somehow the guard managed to pull his gun and shoot, hitting his adversary squarely in the chest. The second burglar dropped the money and went to his bleeding partner's aid. He dragged his injured friend into a light-colored car hidden in the nearby alley. Both bank robbers escaped.

About 7 miles away, a pair of workmen from the water department had just finished restoring service to a rural neighborhood. "The water was off for about an hour," the senior technician later told the police. "We got it running at about 8:55, then stopped for a cup of coffee. We were just heading back when Mike spotted this guy in a field. It was a full moon and we could see he was dragging something through the weeds. We pulled over to see if he needed help. And then we saw the body. He was dragging this dead, bloody body. This guy was little and didn't have a gun. So Bill held him while I phoned the police. That was like 9:25."

"We arrived at 9:31," Officer Brill explained. "The man identified himself as Wally Heath. The body had a bullet in its chest, but Mr. Heath didn't have any explanation to offer. He invited us into his house. Mr. Heath, as it happens, lives right beside the field. The house was furnished nicely but kind of messy. He said his wife had recently left him, run off with some traveling salesman. He seemed more preoccupied with telling us about his domestic situation than about this body. We were there for maybe 10 minutes. Just before we took him in, the washing machine timer went off. We went with him to check it and saw the clothes in the washer were kind of dingy, like they'd been sitting in dirty water. We advised him not to touch them, just in case there might be some evidence. Then we read him his rights."

When the case came to trial, Wallace Heath stood accused of robbery, not murder. The corpse he had been dragging through the field has been identified as the late Judd Okan, a career criminal with a rap sheet in burglary and larceny. Computer-enhanced "stills" from the surveillance camera identified him as the unmasked burglar shot by the security guard. A still of the other robber remained unhelpful. Although the masked image did resemble Wally Heath in general size and build, it also resembled hundreds of other local men.

In court, Wally Heath's attorney seems at a loss.

DEFENSE: My client has absolutely no criminal record. He has lived in this town for 8 years, held the same job for 7 and was married to the same woman for 12. Although the Heaths were not a particularly sociable couple, Mr. Heath has been known to be a law-abiding man with the patience of a saint. He was at home the entire night in question, watching TV and doing his laundry.

True, Mr. Heath is not willing to tell us how he happened across Judd Okan or why he was dragging the body through the field behind his house. But it is not the Defense's job to establish Wally Heath's innocence. Rather, it is the Prosecution's job to establish his guilt, something they will be unable to do.

You and your fellow jurors are also at a loss. If Heath is so innocent, then why won't he explain his incriminating behavior?

Trial Witnesses & Evidence

This crime can be solved with 2 clues.

Evidence Secured in Field

OFFICER: The field covers about 2 acres. Bordering the field on two adjacent sides is a road that swings around. On the third side is the Heath house and on the fourth is an abandoned well with a patch of woods behind it. The tall weeds left good impressions. It was easy to spot the path of trampled weeds. It appeared that a body had been dragged from the road into the middle of the field. We found the body about midway along this path. It was face up, the feet pointing toward the road.

PROSECUTION CROSS-EXAMINATION: What makes you think this path had been made by the dragged body?

OFFICER: We found blood and fibers along the entire path. They all match those of Judd Okan.

Prosecution Exhibit C, Autopsy Report

AUTOPSY REPORT: Cause of death was a single gunshot wound to the chest. The bullet entered the thorax cavity between the third and fourth ribs, causing a collapsed lung and piercing the septum wall between the left and right ventricles. Death occurred within 5 to 10 minutes.

PROSECUTION: Was the bullet in Mr. Okan fired from the handgun belonging to the Ajax Security Co. guard?

DEFENSE OBJECTION: The medical examiner is not a ballistics expert.

The Prosecution's next witness, a ballistics expert, testifies that the bullet did indeed come from the security guard's gun.

Evidence from Car

DEFENSE: Officer, please describe the car that was parked by the field.

OFFICER: It was a tan Toyota registered to the defendant. It was parked on the road beside the path of trodden-down weeds. The Toyota's trunk was open and inside was a shovel. No dirt was visible on the shovel or in the trunk; so, we assumed the implement had not been used recently.

PROSECUTION: Was Mr. Heath's car searched for blood, fiber, hair, dirt, etc.?

OFFICER: Yes, it was.

PROSECUTION: And the results?

OFFICER: There was no blood of any kind. No dirt or vege-tation. We did find several hairs matching the defendant's and fibers matching his clothes. Also, several unidentified hairs and fibers. But we found nothing at all matching the late Mr. Okan.

Laundry Analysis, Defense Witness

The Defense introduces a chemist who analyzed the dirty clothing in Wally Heath's washing machine.

CHEMIST: I started by comparing the dirt in the washer to soil samples from the field.

DEFENSE: And the result?

CHEMIST: No match.

DEFENSE: Were you ever able to match the dirt samples from the clothes?

CHEMIST: As a matter of fact, yes. I discovered from the county that there had been a water-main break that evening. When the water was turned back on at 8:55, it ran dirty for the first several minutes. If Mr. Heath had started the wash cycle at 8:55 or soon after, he would have filled the machine with that dirty water. The samples match perfectly.

Evidence from Defendant's House

DEFENSE: Did you examine the house for clothing?

INVESTIGATING OFFICER: Yes, and we found nothing resem-bling the light-colored jumpsuit worn by the masked per-petrator.

DEFENSE: Would you expect the perpetrator's clothing to have blood on it?

INVESTIGATING OFFICER: Yes. Judd Okan was bleeding heavily. The other man would certainly have gotten it on himself.

DEFENSE: And did you find any blood at all in Mr. Heath's house?

INVESTIGATING OFFICER: We did.

DEFENSE: What? You did?!

INVESTIGATING OFFICER: Yes. We ran over the entire house with phosphorescent light, designed to reveal the smallest traces of blood. We found blood residue on the floor of the laundry room and the kitchen and trailing out into the field.

The Defense appears devastated by this revelation.

The Haunted House Murder

THE PROSECUTOR PACED in front of the jury.

PROSECUTION: It all began as a harmless escapade.

Four healthy teenagers sneaking into an old abandoned house. A final night of adventure before one of them went off to college. That will never happen now. Lilly Kincaid will never go to Princeton. For on that night, Lilly was brutally murdered by this man, William Willis.

Even dressed up in a cheap suit paid for by his lawyer, Billy Willis looked like the homeless recluse he was. Harmless enough, or so everyone had thought.

The prosecutor reviewed the facts. The trespassing teens had been Lilly Kincaid, her younger sister, Anne, and their boyfriends, Mark and Larry. On a sultry August night, a week before Lilly's departure for Princeton, all four finally did what they'd always talked about, breaking into the eerily isolated Alway mansion at midnight and searching for ghosts.

Lilly's boyfriend, Mark, had been in the lead, using his flashlight to illuminate cobweb-filled crannies. Despite promises to the contrary, the boys were having their fun, scaring the girls at every opportunity. They had finished exploring the first floor and were halfway down a second-floor corridor when Larry turned around and saw that Lilly was no longer behind him.

"Lilly? Where are you?" Their whispers grew louder as they began to backtrack along the corridor. "Stop fooling around." Lilly was hardly the type to wander off on her own. "Lilly?" And then they heard it. Several muffled shouts followed by a piercing scream. Lilly's scream.

When Anne and the boys stepped into the dusty bedroom, they saw the 18-year-old stretched out on the bed frame. A hunting knife was protruding from her chest, the black handle-grip facing her shoes. They were hoping it was all a perverse joke, Lilly getting even with the boys. Anne nudged her sister, telling her to cut out the dramatics. "Lilly?" Anne gazed down at her own hands. They were covered in blood. "She's . . .

she's dead."

Mark was just stepping forward to check her pulse when Anne gasped. "Oh, my God. Did you see?" She pointed out into the hallway. "A man with a knife."

Instinctively, the boys gave chase, inadvertently leaving the surviving sister alone. No more than 30 seconds later, as they pursued clouds of cobwebs through the downstairs rooms, a second scream brought them up short. "Anne!" Mark and Larry instantly reversed their tracks.

"You left me alone!" Anne screamed as they ran back in. "Let's get out of here." The boys agreed. Whoever had done this was still close by, wielding a second knife. They ran, Anne sandwiched between her protectors, and didn't stop until they'd reached the safety of the police station.

When Ben Alway, the mansion owner, was told of the murder, his opinion was unequivocal. "Billy Willy," he replied. "Willis, I mean. A homeless drunk who's been squatting in the house for years. I kick him out and lock up the place, but he always finds some way in. The girl must have surprised old Billy. He's got a crazy, violent streak. Anyone'll tell you."

An hour later, the police discovered the lanky, middle-aged drunk passed out in the park. He had finished two pints of bourbon and his hand was gripped around a third. Through his alcoholic stupor, Billy denied the murder. "I ain't been in that place for days. That Alway guy is crazy. Last time, he took a shotgun and put it right up to my head. Said he'd blow my brains out if I ever came back."

Anne Kincaid was unable to identify Billy Willis in a line-up, but there still seemed to be more than enough evidence. The district attorney summed up his case with an emotional appeal.

PROSECUTION: Lilly Kincaid was the proverbial golden girl, the joy of her family, the focus of their hopes and dreams. For years Lilly's parents struggled so that one of their children could go to a good college. And now those hopes and dreams . . . where are they? Stabbed through the heart by a drunken monster.

Trial Witnesses & Evidence

This crime can be solved with 3 clues.

Prosecution Witness, Ben Alway

The Prosecution calls Ben Alway to testify about his meeting with Billy Willis on the day of the murder.

The short, unassuming man says he never threatened Willis with a shotgun and that Willis, a vagrant, appeared edgy and desperate for a drink. During Defense cross-examination, Alway states that on the night of the murder he was at home, 2 blocks away, alone, watching television. The Defense questions Alway about his connection to the victim. Alway teaches at the local high school.

BEN ALWAY: I never had Lilly in any regular class. But in the summer, I work with students, preparing them for college boards. Last year, I coached Lilly, and this summer, Anne was in my group. Now that Lilly is dead, the Kincaids are hoping Anne will get into Princeton.

Defense Witness, Clerk

Vincent Winters, a clerk at All-Nite Liquor, testifies that at approximately 11 P.M. on the night of the murder, Billy Willis entered his store and bought 3 pints of Retcher's bourbon.

VINCENT WINTERS: He paid in loose change, like always. During the day Billy panhandles along Oak Street. Every now and then he makes enough to splurge on bourbon.

The Defense introduces this testimony in an attempt to strengthen the defendant's alibi, that he had been drunk and in the park at the time of the murder.

Police Crime Scene Report

SERGEANT JACKSON (*referring to his notes*): It was a single, fatal blow, delivered in a downward thrust, the handle-grip turned up in the fingers for a better grasp. We have yet to determine ownership of the weapon. The defendant's prints were found in six different locations around the room.

During Defense cross-examination Jackson admits he found no prints on the weapon.

DEFENSE: Isn't it odd for a killer to carefully wipe off the knife and yet leave his prints all around the room?

SERGEANT JACKSON: Maybe.

DEFENSE: Could the defendant have left his prints there a day earlier? Even a week earlier?

SERGEANT JACKSON: I suppose.

DEFENSE: Did any of the defendant's prints contain traces of the victim's blood?

SERGEANT JACKSON: No.

Forensic Blood Report

Under cross-examination, the police expert admits that more than one blood type was found at the scene.

POLICE EXPERT: Our initial sampling produced only one, a type matching the decedent's. A later sample taken from the shirt, however, revealed a secondary blood source. According to tests, this was animal blood, probably chicken.

DEFENSE: Do you have any idea how chicken blood might have gotten to the scene of the crime?

POLICE EXPERT: No idea at all. Unless the lab made a mistake. It happens.

Defense Exhibit A, the Second Knife

A hunting knife, identical in make to the murder weapon, was discovered lodged in the branches of a tree not far from the window of the room where the murder victim was found. Most of the knife's 6-inch blade had been broken off, leaving only a ¾-inch steel shaft. The blade was never found. This second knife had been wiped clean, but a microscopic examination revealed traces of blood on the broken shaft. Lab analysis verified that this was animal blood, probably from a chicken.

The Defense introduces the knife as contradictory evidence, but suggests no plausible theory about how the knife blade had been broken or where the blood came from.

A Witless Eyewitness?

ALICE GABRIEL WAS a lonely woman who liked to use her binoculars to observe the world from her living-room window. Then one afternoon, while scanning the building across the street, Alice got more than she bargained for. Her statement was read in court.

ALICE GABRIEL: Several weeks ago, two unsavory-looking men moved into the dilapidated house directly across from my place. A tall, thin man and a short, fat one, like the Mutt and Jeff characters you read about in crime books. Sometimes a third man would come over. He looked different, nice and mild-mannered. All three often talked or played cards. Sometimes the nice-looking man took notes in a little notepad.

Well, on this particular Sunday, the nice man came to visit again. Only the short fellow was at home and he seemed very drunk. They talked for a while, then got into some sort of argument. All of a sudden the short man pulled out a tiny silver gun and started waving it around. The nice man managed to grab it from him. Then they moved out of my line of sight and I had to change windows. I heard the shot. It wasn't very loud. At the next window, I refocused my binoculars. The short man was grabbing his chest and falling, blood all over his shirt. The nice man was holding the gun. He looked stunned. This was about 5:25 P.M.

A few seconds afterwards, the tall guy came home. He and the killer tried to revive the short guy, but you could tell he was dead. Then the two guys closed the blinds; so, I couldn't see anymore. I ran right into my bedroom and called the police. Believe it or not, I was put on hold for 10 full minutes before someone took down my information and another 7 minutes before a patrol car arrived.

According to police, the body of Sol "Little Sonny" Walker was discovered a half-hour later, not in the house itself but two blocks away, in an alley behind a neighborhood bar. Based on

Alice Gabriel's testimony, the mild-mannered man, Wade Poe, was arrested. A nitric acid test showed that he had recently fired a gun. The tall man of the trio, Busby Berkoff, was arrested as an accessory after the fact, for trying to help Poe cover up the crime and dispose of the body.

The district attorney expected the Defense to enter a plea of self-defense or accidental homicide. But the defendant surprised everyone by claiming total innocence. As the Defense begins its opening argument, you immediately see its line of attack—the credibility of the case's eyewitness.

DEFENSE: Alice Gabriel is a woman desperate for attention and blessed with a vivid imagination. Just look at the holes in her story. She says the victim was wearing a white T-shirt, yet his body was found in a brown dress shirt. She says he was killed by a small silver pistol, yet forensic evidence will show the murder weapon to be a .45-caliber weapon, a much larger gun which was never found. Even her statement on the time of death is wrong. Alice Gabriel says the shot occurred at 5:25. Yet we will produce two other witnesses who set the time of the shot at 5:40. Most important of all, Miss Gabriel says Sol Walker was shot in his house. Yet the police's own evidence proves that his murder took place in the alley behind McGregor's bar. Ladies and gentlemen, after hearing all the evidence, you will have no choice but to disregard Miss Gabriel's testimony and find my client not guilty.

Trial Witnesses & Evidence

This crime can be solved with 2 clues.

Defense Witness, McGregor's Bartender

BARTENDER: At about 5:35 P.M., Busby Berkoff walked in and ordered a double of my best scotch.

DEFENSE: Did he seem upset, like his friend had just been shot?

BARTENDER: No. He was in a great mood, happier than I seen him in a while. He and Sol live nearby. They'd been depressed lately on account of their shaky finances.

DEFENSE: And when did you hear the gunshot?

BARTENDER: About 5:40. Busby and I both heard it. I couldn't leave the bar and Busby didn't feel safe checking it on his own. This ain't the best neighborhood. So, we called the cops.

Defense Witness, Mrs. Wade Poe

MRS. WADE POE: Wade first met Sonny and Busby at McGregor's bar. Normally, Wade would never associate with that type, but Wade is a novelist. He's writing a book about low-lifes and con artists and wanted it to sound authentic. That's why he befriended them—for research.

PROSECUTION CROSS-EXAMINATION: Are you aware that at 5:32 on the day of the murder, your husband went to the bank beside McGregor's bar and withdrew $10,000?

MRS. WADE POE: That's what the police say.

PROSECUTION: Do you know why he withdrew it?

MRS. WADE POE: No.

PROSECUTION: Do you know what happened to that money?

MRS. WADE POE: No, I don't.

PROSECUTION: Could he have used it to buy Busby Berkoff's silence?

DEFENSE: Objection.

JUDGE: Withdraw the question.

PROSECUTION: Does your husband own a gun, Mrs. Poe?

MRS. WADE POE: He used to own an old Colt .45. I don't know what happened to it. Wade says it was stolen.

Police Chemist

PROSECUTION: Did you perform a nitric acid test on the defendant?

POLICE CHEMIST: Yes. It showed that he had recently fired a gun.

PROSECUTION: Did you perform the test on anyone else?

POLICE CHEMIST: Yes. On the deceased, Busby Berkoff, Mrs. Wade Poe, the bartender, and Ms. Gabriel.

PROSECUTION: The results?

POLICE CHEMIST: Minute traces of nitrates were found on the deceased's right hand and in his right trouser pocket. Nothing on the others.

DEFENSE CROSS-EXAMINATION: Is it possible to pick up gunpowder traces if you simply handle a fired gun, without actually firing it yourself?

POLICE CHEMIST: Yes, but . . .

DEFENSE: Can gunpowder nitrates be washed off?

POLICE CHEMIST: If you wash thoroughly, yes.

DEFENSE: And if the assailant were wearing gloves?

POLICE CHEMIST: Then, of course, there would be no nitrate traces at all.

Prosecution Witness, Forensic Expert

PROSECUTION: You examined evidence from both scenes. Please summarize your findings.

FORENSIC EXPERT: In Mr. Walker's living room, we used a phosphorescent scope and found no blood traces. Nor was there any other evidence indicating a crime had taken place. In the alley behind the bar, we found quite a bit of blood, all matching the deceased's. The spatter patterns indicate the body had not been moved and that this was the scene of the crime.

DEFENSE: Here is the report of the first officer to arrive at Mr. Walker's home. Please read this section out loud.

FORENSIC EXPERT (READING): "The room was stuffy, and when I first entered I smelled a little gunpowder."

DEFENSE: Do you still insist there was no evidence of a murder having been committed there?

FORENSIC EXPERT: Yes. The officer was undoubtedly mistaken.

Autopsy Report

MEDICAL EXAMINER (READING): "Mr. Walker was killed by a single shot entering the chest cavity just below the sternum. His assailant had been facing him, approximately 8 feet away. The bullet we retrieved was from a .45-caliber handgun. Death occurred within seconds."

PROSECUTION: Was the physical evidence more consistent with an act of self-defense or with cold-blooded murder?

MEDICAL EXAMINER: Impossible to tell. We certainly found nothing to indicate that Mr. Walker had been threatening his assailant. But I really can't draw any conclusions.

Death & the Single Girl

Paul Gruber had been living in Casanova Towers for about two years and something always seemed to be going wrong. When he came home from work Tuesday evening, his new roommate was in the bathroom mopping up a puddle of water. "It started 15 minutes ago," Archie explained. "I pounded on the door of the apartment upstairs. No one's home. And the doorman's not answering the intercom."

Paul looked up at the bathroom ceiling. Water was dripping between the seams of the cheap acoustic tiles. "Ginger Mint's apartment."

"Didn't she give you a key for emergencies?" Archie asked.

"Yeah. I hope nothing's wrong."

Paul and Archie walked up one flight. Paul knocked on the door, then finally flipped through his keys, finding the one labeled Ginger.

"Inside her place it was deadly quiet," Paul later told the police. "Archie turned one way, to the bathroom. I turned the other, to the bedroom. Ginger's body was behind the bed; so, it took me a little while to see it. I called out. As soon as Archie came and saw the blood, he started to heave. He was heaving so hard he popped a button on his shirt. Archie wanted to look around for it, but I said no.

"On the way out of the apartment, I heard water running. I went into the bathroom and turned off the sink taps. I know I shouldn't have touched anything, but I didn't want the flooding to get worse."

Ginger Mint had moved to town 6 months ago and became involved with Todd Iona, a movie projectionist. On the day of the murder, Ginger told a coworker that she was nervous. Her boyfriend was going to drop over that evening. She was hoping to end their tempestuous relationship once and for all and wasn't sure how he would react.

Todd Iona is sitting at the Defense table as the Prosecutor previews the case against him.

PROSECUTION: We will introduce witnesses who will testify to

Mr. Iona's jealous rages. Indeed, the victim told friends they were going to be meeting that night and she was afraid. Iona arrived at Ginger's prepared for murder. It took him only a minute to do it, using a knife from the kitchen. We will show how, after brutally stabbing her to death, Iona set up the bathroom sink to overflow, knowing that this would cause the body to be discovered. And why did he want it discovered so quickly? Because at that particular moment Todd Iona had an alibi.

Mr. Iona, you see, was a projectionist in a movie theater only a few steps from Casanova Towers. Between changing reels, he had 20 minutes, plenty of time to sneak out and run through the apartment tower's rear entrance, using the key Ms. Mint had given him just a month before. Minutes later, he was back in the privacy of his booth, where he had another full hour before his break, all the time he needed to clean up and dispose of his bloody clothing.

DEFENSE (*sarcastic*): What bloody clothing? Was any blood at all found in the projection booth or on my client? No. Ms. Mint did not ask my client to her apartment that evening. Why would she? He was working. No one saw him leave the theater or enter Casanova Towers. And as for having access, so what? The doorman had keys to her apartment. So did her downstairs neighbor. All the Prosecution has is the hearsay of a friend who said Ms. Mint was meeting her boyfriend. Is that enough evidence to convict a man of murder? I think not.

Trial Witnesses & Evidence

This murder can be solved with 2 clues.

Officer on Scene, Bedroom

OFFICER: No liftable prints, other than Ms. Mint's, were obtained from the bedroom.

PROSECUTION: Did anything in the

bedroom catch your attention?

OFFICER: We discovered a white button on the rug between the body and the wall. This proved to be from Archie Gill's shirt. In addition, we found a photograph, a torn photograph. It was hidden behind a framed picture of Ms. Mint on the bureau. It showed Ms. Mint, presumably posed beside another person who had been torn out of the picture. We tried to trace it but haven't had any luck.

The partial photograph is admitted into evidence. It shows Ginger standing in the snow with a man's arm around her shoulder. In the background is a lighted Christmas tree.

Prosecution Witness, Ginger's Coworker

GINGER'S COWORKER: I met Ginger when she moved here in April, 6 months ago. She wasn't very talkative, but every now and then she'd mention Todd and how possessive he was.

DEFENSE CROSS-EXAMINATION: Did Ms. Mint say it was Mr. Iona who was coming over that night?

GINGER'S COWORKER: No. She just said "my boyfriend." She might have said "ex-boyfriend" once. I don't remember.

DEFENSE: So, she could have been expecting someone other than Mr. Iona.

GINGER'S COWORKER: I guess. Ginger didn't talk a lot about her love life.

Officer on Scene, Bathroom

OFFICER: Prints matching the deceased's were found all over the bathroom. Prints matching the accused's were found on the counter and mirror. A different set of prints was lifted from the sink's faucet handles. These were matched with those of Paul Gruber. A wad of toilet paper had been stuffed into the sink's overflow drain, which forced the water to pour out onto the floor.

DEFENSE CROSS-EXAMINATION: If Mr. Iona had visited the

deceased's apartment within the past few days, wouldn't you expect to find his prints in the bathroom?

OFFICER: Yes, I suppose so.

Prosecution Witness, Doorman

DOORMAN: Ms. Mint came in at 6:15 P.M. She said she was expecting a guest within the hour. I know Mr. Iona. She didn't mention him by name.

PROSECUTION: Did any guest arrive by the main door?

DOORMAN: No. And I was on the desk from 6:15 right up until 7:20. That's when Mr. Gruber called down and told me the police were coming.

DEFENSE CROSS-EXAMINATION: You were on the desk from 6:15 to 7:20?

DOORMAN: That's right.

DEFENSE: Mr. Gruber's roommate, Archie Gill, says he called the front desk at about 7:10 and no one answered.

DOORMAN: Well, I was there. Maybe I stepped outside in front for a smoke or something.

Prosecution Witness, Maintenance Man

PROSECUTION: Will you describe what you discovered in the garbage the morning after the murder?

MAINTENANCE MAN: Well, something was clogging the garbage chute. I went up floor by floor until I found the clog. It was between the fourth and fifth floors.

PROSECUTION: Ms. Mint lived on the fifth floor?

MAINTENANCE MAN: Right. Anyway, I found three large towels, all sopping wet. That's what was blocking the chute. On top of the towels was a pair of gloves. This particular hall chute runs right beside the murdered woman's apartment; so, I knew better than to touch anything.

The black leather gloves are admitted into evidence. They're men's large, the same size worn by the accused.

The Vanishing Verrocchio

Lord George, the sixteenth earl of Brighton, had amassed one of the finest private collections of Renaissance art in Great Britain. A notorious recluse, the earl rarely ventured off his estate and hardly ever allowed outside eyes to view his priceless works. Like many collectors, he was obsessed with increasing his holdings. When it was announced that the Augustinian Fathers were considering selling their Verrocchio bust of St. Augustine, the earl jumped at the chance, claiming that he was prepared to offer more than any museum to acquire the statue, one of the few by Leonardo da Vinci's famous teacher to survive the centuries.

Late one afternoon, a black van drove through the gates of Brighton Manor, bringing the bronze St. Augustine for a formal appraisal and perhaps an informal offer. The earl of Brighton met his overnight guests at the door. Father Damien, a grim-visaged man, introduced himself. "Lord George, I must warn you. I am opposed to this transaction. The bust was a gift to our order centuries ago from the artist himself. To sell it would be a grave sacrilege."

The earl stood tall and unmoved. "That's your opinion. Don't tell me you drove the statue all the way here in that van? What about security?"

"The Lord is our security," Damien replied. "And Father Vito." He pointed to his companion, a priest about the same imposing size as himself but with a fierce scar running across one cheek.

The two friars carried a wooden crate through the hall and into the library and carefully unveiled the life-size bust. "Stunning," a voice whispered from the shadows. "Oh. Sorry to startle." A plump man waddled forward. "I'm Warren Tuffet, auction-house appraiser. Lord George brought me in to authenticate and advise. It's the Verrocchio, all right," he added after a minute's worth of inspection.

The foursome left the statue in the protection of an aging guard while the host led his guests on a tour. "The house has a Catholic background, you'll be pleased to hear. The second earl of Brighton was a devout Roman Catholic. During the reign of Henry VIII, he took in several priests, hiding them from the king's wrath. I assume you want to see my collection," he added reluctantly and showed them into the exhibition rooms.

When the museum tour was over, the host and his guests retired to refresh themselves and dress for dinner. It was during this break, while all were alone in different parts of the manor, that the crime took place.

At 7:17 P.M., the butler walked by the library and discovered the guard stumbling groggily about. The Verrocchio was missing from its wooden stand. Immediately, the servant sounded the alarm. Within minutes, the entire household had assembled. "Got hit," the guard mumbled, massaging a welt on the back of his head. "Knocked me down but not out. I saw . . ."

"Saw what?" Warren Tuffet demanded. "Who took the statue?"

The old guard, Edgar Chipping, didn't answer. He was too busy clutching his arm, then his chest, and then collapsing to the parquet floor under the impact of a massive heart attack. "Priest stole."

"Priest?" Lord George shouted. "Which priest? Both of them?"

"No." The guard shook his head in frustration, his face growing beet-red. "Priest stole." He pointed toward Father Damien standing by the spot where the statue had rested. "Here. Understand."

Those were to be the last words Edgar Chipping uttered. Within seconds he was dead, leaving Father Damien to face one count of grand larceny and one count of felony murder. The statue was never found and two months later the Augustinian was brought to trial, accused by the last words of a dying man.

Trial Witnesses & Evidence

This crime can be solved with 2 clues.

Prosecution Witness, Security Chief
The earl's security chief describes Brighton Manor's antitheft precautions.

SECURITY CHIEF: The exhibition rooms are under constant video surveillance with several alarms spaced throughout, protecting the more valuable pieces. Unfortunately, there was no camera in the library, but we did have one focused on the manor's front door. It was operational at the time of the theft. As for the wall surrounding the grounds, it's made of smooth stone, 10 feet high and topped with barbed wire.

The videotape of the manor's front door is admitted into evidence.

Prosecution Exhibit A, Videotape
A videotape of the manor's front entrance reveals this: At 7:09 P.M., a tall figure dressed in an Augustinian friar's traveling robe with a hooded cape is seen exiting. Still photographs taken from the tape show that the figure is fully masked by his hood and robe and carrying a cloth sack filled with a heavy, bulky object.

There is no video record of anyone reentering the manor through the front door. The police assume that if the figure reentered the manor house, it was through another door. Several other doors had been unlocked at the time.

Officer at Scene
PROSECUTION: When you searched the area directly outside the grounds, what did you find?
OFFICER: Directly behind the west wall, the wall closest to the manor house, we discovered a large cloth sack, similar

to the one in the video. Inside it was a hooded cape and a black robe.

PROSECUTION: Were you able to determine ownership of the robe?

OFFICER: It belonged to Father Damien—his traveling robe.

PROSECUTION: Do you have a theory of how the sack came to be found there?

OFFICER: Our theory is that Father Damien handed it over the wall to an accomplice who removed the statue, leaving the sack, robe, and hood.

DEFENSE CROSS-EXAMINATION: Why would Father Damien throw something as incriminating as his robe over the wall?

OFFICER: I don't know.

Defense Witness, Butler

DEFENSE: Was anything other than the Verrocchio statue missing from the library?

BUTLER: Yes, a Chinese pot. About 2 feet high. Fairly valuable. It had been standing in a corner of the room for years.

DEFENSE: Do you know what happened to the pot?

BUTLER: The police found it on the lawn, somewhere between the manor house and the west wall. It was still in one piece, thank heavens.

Statements of Whereabouts during Crime

LORD GEORGE: I was in my study. I had decided to make an offer on the Verrocchio and was calculating the range of my bid.

FATHER DAMIEN: I was in the guest room, in prayer. I was praying that the statue not be taken from us.

WARREN TUFFET: The butler will probably tell you I was sneaking around the upper floors. True. This was my first time inside the manor. Even though we had been given a tour, I was anxious to wander through at my own pace, appreciating the grand old house.

FATHER VITO: I was in my room on the phone. I was telephoning an old acquaintance in the city. I had heard a serious rumor regarding Lord George's financial solvency and asked my friend to do a little checking.

No Brake for the Wearys

THE DISTRICT ATTORNEY points at the defendant, a handsome man in his twenties.

PROSECUTION: For years, Adam Weary had been living off his father's millions. And then the money dried up. Adam's new stepmother finally persuaded her husband to stop supporting Adam's spendthrift ways. Adam's art gallery was in desperate need of funds in order to survive, money he could no longer get from his father. And that is why, on May 15, Adam Weary coldly planned and executed the double murder of his father and stepmother.

The Prosecution's case seemed solid. After the elderly executive George Weary married Pauline Gibson, the young beauty immediately took control of their finances, redecorating the hillside mansion and cutting off George's monetary outlays to his son.

Adam had tried many jobs during his young life: restaurateur, film producer, artist, and, finally, owner of an art gallery. Each project had been lavishly subsidized by an indulgent father until Pauline came along. Despite this new development, Adam remained the secondary heir, inheriting the entire Weary fortune if both George and his new wife died.

According to the Defense's opening statement, Adam drove over to the hillside mansion on the morning of May 15 for breakfast. While there, Adam claims, Pauline asked him to change the oil in George's Cadillac. It seems the millionaire refused to go to the expense of a professional oil change and usually did the job himself. But Pauline was worried that George was getting too old for such exertion and might injure himself. Adam readily agreed, changing the Cadillac's oil and leaving the mansion at 11 A.M., just as a light, steady rain began to fall.

Adam's parting words were to remind Pauline about his gallery reception. He was counting on both of them to come that afternoon at 2. From the mansion, Adam drove straight to his gallery, where he remained until he was informed of the deaths.

At 5 P.M. Pauline's friend Sissy Yonkers dialed 911. "Something must have happened," she told the emergency operator. "Pauline was supposed to be at my place at 4 to go shopping. She's never late. She was going to drive here directly from the gallery, and her husband was going to drive to the airport to catch a business flight to Dallas. I telephoned his son's gallery. Neither one of them ever showed up. They've been missing for hours."

The 911 operator took down the report but did not share what he already knew, that the Wearys weren't missing, they were dead. At 1:30 that afternoon, George's Cadillac had flown through a guardrail and plummeted to the bottom of a ravine half a mile down the hill from the mansion. The plush leather and wood interior held the mangled remains of George and Pauline Weary. A later inspection of the vehicle showed that the brake lines had been neatly severed.

Although fingerprints had been wiped clean from the area around the brakes, clear sets of Adam Weary's prints were found on other parts of the underchassis.

The district attorney concluded his opening statement.

PROSECUTION: Only Adam Weary had a motive; no one else profited from their deaths. Only Adam had opportunity; he was the only outsider admitted into the Weary home that morning. And although Adam will tell you his flimsy, unbelievable story about being asked to change his father's oil for the first time in his life, you will find that only Adam Weary had the means to commit these murders, since only his prints are to be found under the car.

Trial Witnesses & Evidence

This crime can be solved with 2 clues.

Medical Examiner's Testimony

MEDICAL EXAMINER: Despite the air-
bags, both decedents were killed on
impact. George Weary was in the driv-
er's seat wearing a seat belt. His
wounds were consistent with those expected: a broken neck
and spine, other nonlethal fractures, and multiple contu-
sions. Pauline Weary had not been wearing a seat belt. Her
wounds also included a broken spine and were generally
consistent with those expected.

On Defense cross-examination, the coroner admits that one
of Pauline's wounds is not consistent with the crash: a severe
open contusion on the back of her head. The ecchymosis (dis-
coloration and swelling) indicates this wound had been in-
flicted before Pauline Weary's death. Also, white gravel fragments were imbedded in the wound.

The medical examiner also reported that the back of the
decedent's dress was wet and dirty and contained white gravel
fragments.

Police Crime Scene Report

A homicide detective testifies that no empty oilcans or other
evidence of an oil change were found in the Wearys' garage.

DEFENSE: What other findings can you report from your examination of the garage and the grounds?

HOMICIDE DETECTIVE: We found a patch of spilled oil on
the garage floor in the spot where the Cadillac had been
parked. The fingerprints of the accused were not found on
the other car in the garage, Pauline Weary's Porsche. The
brakes on the Porsche had not been tampered with. Blood
was discovered on the white gravel path, halfway between

the mansion and the garage. The gravel had been disturbed around that spot.

Defense Exhibit A, Prenuptial Agreement

The Defense introduces into evidence the prenuptial agreement between George and Pauline Weary, witnessed and signed a month before their marriage. In the document Pauline gave up all claims to community property and agreed, in the event of a divorce, to a lump settlement of $200,000.

The Defense introduced this evidence in an attempt to show that the Weary marriage was fragile from the beginning and unlikely to last.

Prosecution Exhibit C, George Weary's Will

Hoping to clearly establish a motive, the Prosecution asked the Weary lawyer to read aloud the provisions of George Weary's will, drafted a week after his marriage. In the will, George Weary left the bulk of his estate to his wife, Pauline. In the event of her death before the will could be probated, Pauline's portion of the estate would revert to George's previous heir, his only child, Adam Weary.

Defense Exhibit B, Receipt from Car Interior

The Defense, in an attempt to establish an alibi for the time of the brake tampering, introduces a receipt found crumpled in the ashtray of the wrecked Cadillac. The receipt, for a quart of milk and a carton of cigarettes, is from a convenience store located at the bottom of the hill near the Weary estate. It was stamped at 11:48 A.M. on May 15, the day of the murder. The Defense uses this receipt to demonstrate that someone used the Cadillac after Adam left the house and that the brakes must have been in working order at that time.

The Prosecution introduces the salesclerk on duty at the convenience store at the time. She says she cannot remember either the sale or the car. The Prosecution claims that the receipt had been fabricated and planted in the Cadillac to provide Adam Weary with an alibi.

Trial of the Black Widow

For two months, the exclusive community of Palm Bay has been obsessed with a murder that many of its most influential citizens actually witnessed. You and your eleven colleagues feel lucky to sit here every day and weigh the evidence against this beautiful, and, some might add, deadly woman of the world.

It was less than a year ago that Anabel Lee moved to Palm Bay, renting a tastefully expensive beach house. A vivacious and stunning woman, Anabel quickly made friends, especially with Victor Ricolah, next-door neighbor and retired financier. They were engaged within two months, married within three. In his opening statement, the district attorney outlines the events of Victor's final garden party of the season, his last garden party ever.

The festivities were in full swing on that sunny afternoon when the host asked his wife to fetch him a drink. Anabel had just sent the bartender off for more limes; so, she made it herself, expertly mixing the gin and tonic and adding ice from an electric ice cooler plugged into an outlet in the gazebo. She tasted the drink, pronounced it delicious, then handed the glass to Victor, who used a paper napkin to wipe a red gash of lipstick off the rim before drinking.

That was the last contact that Anabel had with her husband. For the next half-hour, Victor sipped his drink, munched on a catered buffet of overpriced delectables, and chatted with his neighbors. At one point he borrowed a cigarette from his best friend and tennis partner, Keith Brown, but smoked only half before stubbing it out.

When Victor collapsed on the lawn clutching his throat, no one even imagined poison, except the poisoner of course. Three plastic surgeons and a dermatologist made vain attempts to revive him. And all this while the servants were busy washing glasses and disposing of whatever evidence might have existed of the murder.

Anabel tried to arrange a quick cremation, but Palm Bay law required an autopsy. The result left no doubt: potassium cyanide, guaranteed to give effective results within a matter of minutes.

PROSECUTION: The Prosecution will show that last month Mrs. Ricolah drove to Boca Raton to purchase an industrial metal cleaner, a clear liquid composed primarily of potassium cyanide. We will also show that this was not the first time Anabel Lee Ricolah, born Amy Long, and also known as Annie Lyons and Andrea Leon, has lost a husband under suspicious circumstances. In at least two previous instances, she married wealthy men. In both of these cases, her husbands died within a year and in both cases their remains were cremated. Anabel Lee is what crime literature calls a "black widow," someone who weds and kills with impunity. It is your job, ladies and gentlemen of the jury, to see that her crime spree stops here.

Anabel's lawyer was dismissive.

DEFENSE: There is no evidence connecting my client to this crime. So, she bought a metal cleaner. She likes a clean house. As for opportunity . . . cyanide is a fast-acting poison. And yet Mrs. Ricolah and her husband had no contact with each other for the last half-hour of his life. Other suspects abound. The Ricolah housekeeper, Emma Peters, had been the deceased's mistress for years before he threw her over for the defendant. The deceased's best friend, Keith Brown, had been an ardent suitor of Anabel's before the marriage. Both Emma Peters and Keith Brown had motives just as compelling as my client's and even greater opportunity.

You get the sinking feeling that no matter who poisoned Victor, there may not be enough evidence to prove it. Still, the question remains: Who killed Victor Ricolah? And how?

Trial Witnesses & Evidence

This crime can be solved in 2 clues.

Prosecution Witness, Toxicologist

TOXICOLOGIST: Luckily, Green Lady Catering uses distinctively colored garbage bags. We were able to recover all the party trash from the dump and sift through it. We limited ourselves to items Mr. Ricolah was observed ingesting. The videotape helped us in that regard. We also checked containers that might have held the poisoned item.

PROSECUTION: And what did you find?

TOXICOLOGIST: We found liquid traces of potassium cyanide inside a plastic food-storage bag—the kind with blue and yellow stripes on top. We also tested a tiny patch of dead grass near the spot where Mr. Ricolah collapsed. Again, we found minute traces of cyanide. In both cases, the chemical composition matched that of a common industrial metal cleaner.

DEFENSE: Objection. Information not asked for.

PROSECUTION: Were the traces of cyanide consistent with the ingredients of the industrial metal cleaner, Exhibit B?

TOXICOLOGIST: Yes.

Prosecution Witness, Housekeeper

Emma Peters, the Ricolah housekeeper, had helped the caterers clean up and was observed disposing of several food storage bags.

PROSECUTION: Do you remember what happened with the storage bags?

EMMA PETERS: As far as I can recall, I threw away three of them, all with those blue and yellow stripes on top. That's the kind Green Lady uses. I buy the same brand for the

Ricolah household. One of the bags came from behind the buffet table. I think they were using it for parsley. The other two came from the bar area in the gazebo. One was used to store garnish items for drinks, and the other I found inside the electric ice cooler.

Prosecution Witness, Caterer

CATERER: Mrs. Ricolah's behavior seemed a little odd that day. For one thing, she insisted on doing many things our staff normally does, things like personally filling the ice cooler and stocking the garnish bins with lemons and limes and cherries. We tried to tell her, diplomatically, that we would take care of those details, but she insisted on doing them herself.

DEFENSE CROSS-EXAMINATION: Did you ever cater for the Ricolah household before?

CATERER: No.

DEFENSE: So, you never worked for Mrs. Ricolah before. In fact, that was the first time you ever met her.

CATERER: That's correct.

DEFENSE: So, you have no way of knowing what her normal behavior was and what might have been odd. In fact, she might normally be an independent person who likes to do things for herself.

CATERER: I suppose.

Cross-Examination, Toxicologist

DEFENSE: You've told the court where you found traces of poison. But where *didn't* you find traces?

TOXICOLOGIST: On everything else.

DEFENSE: You tested the paper napkin with the red lipstick smear? The lipstick tube? The cigarette butts? Dessert canapés? Drinking glasses?

TOXICOLOGIST: No, not the glasses. They had all been washed.

DEFENSE: But you tested everything else I mentioned?

TOXICOLOGIST: Yes.

DEFENSE: And the results of those tests?

TOXICOLOGIST: No trace of poison on any of them.

Defense Exhibit A, Party Videotape

Victor Ricolah had hired a video company to make a tape of the party, thereby ensuring a record of his own demise. By a lucky fluke, the videotape focuses on Victor in the minutes just prior to his death.

VIDEOTAPE: Victor is in the midst of his friends, nursing the last quarter of his gin and tonic. He stubs out his cigarette in an ashtray as Keith Brown deposits a plate of half-eaten food on a table and walks away. Victor absentmindedly eats a potato chip from the plate. Emma Peters passes by with a tray of dessert canapés. Several guests munch on the little sweets, including Victor. Halfway through his first bite, Victor clutches at his throat and collapses, dropping both the canapé and his glass on the lawn. The videotape continues to roll until the arrival of Mrs. Ricolah and the first doctor.

The Hot Designer

Vanushka Designs of New York was the hottest fashion house in the country. Its founder, Vera Vanushka, had led VDNY through eight spectacular years and was reaping the rewards by taking the company public in a sudden stock offering.

The delicate financial negotiations had been hindered by Vanushka's cold. She reportedly caught the bug one afternoon while walking on the beach during a thunderstorm. For several days, she stayed housebound in her Southampton mansion while Manny Moore, her chief financial officer, worked out details with the bankers. Despite her debilitating summer sniffles, the flamboyant designer kept in touch, driving Rose, her personal secretary, nearly crazy with an onslaught of faxes and memos to everyone in the company.

On Monday morning, VDNY made its debut on the stock exchange, soaring $20 from its opening price. But on that same evening a tragic, fatal fire took place and when the market reopened the next day, Tuesday, VDNY stock headed into a nosedive. Not only had Vanushka's charred remains been found among the ruins of her mansion, but Harve Grant, her brilliant assistant, had been arrested for arson and first-degree murder.

The Southampton courthouse was packed as the young, meticulously dressed defendant was led in. He hardly looked like a killer. But, as the prosecution pointed out, Harve certainly had a motive.

PROSECUTION: Harve Grant came to Vanushka fresh from the Fashion Institute. She took a chance with the unproven designer and was rewarded with three years of blockbuster collections. Vera Vanushka was certainly aware of Harve's value, and she made him a promise. Very soon, after the spring collection was shown, she would give him a share in the company. After all, Vanushka's financial officer had a piece; so did Rose, her longtime secretary. When VDNY finally went public, Harve could sell, growing rich with the rest of them. It was a promise Vanushka betrayed. And that betrayal led directly to her murder.

Harve slaved over the new collection, then flew off on vacation. On that fateful Monday morning, he was relaxing on a Mexican beach when he happened to glance at last Friday's *Wall Street Journal*, announcing the upcoming stock sale. Harve grabbed the first plane back to New York, and by that evening had arrived in the Hamptons. We do not know what transpired between Ms. Vanushka and the irate young man. But we do know the result. Harve knocked out the senior designer, left her in the kitchen, and then tinkered with the toaster oven. Five minutes after he left, when the appliance's timer went off, an electrical fire was ignited, fueled by a pile of newspapers on the counter. Harve was counting on the fire to make a cold-blooded murder appear like an accident.

DEFENSE: When my client arrived at the Vanushka home, naturally he was angry. No one answered the bell, the servants having been given two weeks off, so Harve broke a window and let himself in. He wandered around, but Ms. Vanushka didn't seem to be there. It never occurred to him to check the kitchen. His employer was hardly the domestic type. Ten minutes after arriving, at approximately 8:20 P.M., Mr. Grant drove away. Both his arrival and departure times have been documented by observant neighbors. Ten minutes. Hardly enough time to kill a person and arrange the elaborate electrical fire he's accused of having set up.

The evidence is circumstantial at best. The fire left no prints. No proof at all that he'd been in that kitchen. The prosecution cannot even establish the cause of death with complete certainty. For all we know, Ms. Vanushka may have accidentally set the fire herself, then died of a heart attack before she could escape. Stranger things have happened.

Your job is simply to find the defendant guilty or not guilty. Nothing more. But you can't help wondering what really happened that night in Southampton.

Trial Witnesses & Evidence

This crime can be solved with 2 clues.

Prosecution Witness, Ms. Vanushka's Secretary, Rose Clark

ROSE CLARK: I was in the office late that night. Ms. V. called about 8 P.M. She said she was at the house, but from the reception I could tell she was using her cellular phone. Ms. V. used that cell phone a lot. It was a designer model and she was partial to it.

PROSECUTION: Did Ms. Vanushka speak to anyone else?

ROSE CLARK: I'm sure other people in the office heard me talking to her, but no. Since her cold, Ms. V. communicated only through me or through Manny. I'm sure the phone company can supply you with the exact time of the call.

The Prosecution later produces records showing a call from Vera Vanushka's cellular phone to VDNY offices: 7:53 to 8:05 P.M.

Prosecution Witness, Fire Marshal

FIRE MARSHAL: We arrived on the scene at exactly 8:55. The fire was already out of control. I know all the mansions in the area, all the people, too. I called my office and asked them to get in touch with Manny Moore. I figured someone should be notified. He was having a dinner party at his house, maybe 10 minutes away. He came over immediately.

PROSECUTION: Can you describe the kitchen after the fire had been put out?

FIRE MARSHAL: Well, Ms. Vanushka was on the floor, lying on her back, approximately 5 feet from the counter where the toaster oven was situated. It was the most badly burned body I'd ever seen.

PROSECUTION: Did you find Ms. Vanushka's cellular phone anywhere in the room?

FIRE MARSHAL: Yes. We found the blackened remains of a phone right on top of the toaster. It was pretty well toasted—no pun intended. The representative from Nokia was able to identify the model—a custom-made design they'd done exclusively for Ms. Vanushka.

Prosecution Witness, Coroner

CORONER: The body was close to the blaze's center; so, there was a lot of damage. A surprising amount. Massive tissue damage, ruptured eardrums, severe nerve damage, as if they'd been fried. A broken femur. Even cataracts on both corneas. Vera Vanushka had literally been burned to death.

PROSECUTION: Then you would say she had definitely been alive when the fire started?

CORONER: Absolutely.

DEFENSE CROSS-EXAMINATION: For most fire victims, what is the cause of death?

CORONER: In most cases, it's smoke inhalation.

DEFENSE: But Ms. Vanushka didn't die of smoke inhalation; she was burned to death.

CORONER: Correct.

DEFENSE: Could the cause of death have been something other than the fire? Say, a severe electrical shock?

CORONER: Perhaps. But it would have to be extremely severe, more than you could ever get from a toaster oven.

Defense Witness, Phone Company Technician

DEFENSE: The charred cellular phone discovered in the kitchen—can you positively identify that as Ms. Vanushka's?

PHONE TECHNICIAN: The phone was a custom-designed Nokia. There are only two similar instruments in existence, one owned by the defendant and one owned by Manny Moore.

DEFENSE: So, you can't be positive that it was Ms. Vanushka's phone that was burned. It could have been Mr. Moore's or Mr. Grant's.

PHONE TECHNICIAN: Well, normally we can tell by the circuitry or the I.D. code. Both of these were obliterated in the fire.

DEFENSE: So, it could have been one of the other two phones burned in the fire. You really don't know.

PROSECUTION: Objection.

JUDGE: Where is this line of questioning headed?

DEFENSE: The Defense merely wants to show that the call recorded as coming from Ms. Vanushka that night did not necessarily originate from the phone found in her kitchen.

Prosecution Exhibit A, Burned Umbrella

The Prosecution's case was damaged by the coroner's testimony. In the hope of emphasizing the intensity of the fire as the cause of death, the district attorney introduces a beach umbrella that had been stored in a closet just a few feet from the toaster oven. The metal frame is severely scorched, bent from the heat. A fire expert testifies that the umbrella could only have been reduced to that state by an intensely hot fire.

PROSECUTION: And, in your opinion, could such an intense fire kill someone before he or she died of smoke inhalation?

DEFENSE: Objection. Witness is not a medical expert.

JUDGE: Objection sustained.

The Lady in the Dumbwaiter

I T WAS A chilly evening in March, 1930. England's legendary tycoon Lord Dudley was hosting a dinner party at his London mansion. As midnight struck, only the overnight guests remained, sipping their port and admiring the Asprey Whites, a collection of unset diamonds that had been passed down in Lady Dudley's family for generations.

"It will be a pity to sell them," Lady Dudley sighed. "But we do so need the money, at least until this stock-market thing turns around."

Lord Dudley protested that conditions were not that desperate. "How many times must I tell you, dear? I don't want you to do it."

"They're mine and I'm going to. I don't know why you're being so stubborn. Why, just last November, you were begging me to sell."

Marie Dudley was a sensible, good-natured girl, and she seconded her mother's feelings. "Don't keep them for my sake, Daddy. Enough of Gene's money survived the crash. If ever I need diamonds, I'm sure my future husband will provide."

Captain Eugene Batts held a family pedigree even more distinguished than the Dudleys'. "Within reason," the young aristocrat chortled. "Lucky for me, our Marie is not that fond of jewelry."

The fifth and final member of the group raised her voice in disbelief. "What? How can any woman not be fond of jewelry?" Katrina Burghar was Marie Dudley's best friend from school, as daring and full of life as Marie was drab and proper.

Lord Dudley stood by the window smoking his pipe. "What's that?" Suddenly he was gazing into the dark. "I saw something move. In the garden." Captain Batts joined him, and both men stared out into the darkness. "Someone was there, I tell you." The butler was sent out to check but reported that the garden was empty. Whatever had been out there was no longer around.

As the party broke up, Lord Dudley swept the diamonds into their velvet pouch. "I think I'll keep these in my bedroom. Better than the safe. Someone was definitely prowling around."

It was shortly after 1 A.M. when the first gunshot was heard. Lady Dudley emerged from her second-floor boudoir. Captain Batts came down from the third-floor guest bedroom and his fiancée ran up the stairs from the library. All three approached Lord Dudley's suite only to find the door locked.

A second gunshot thundered through the hall and was quickly followed by a dull thud. Mere seconds later, when Captain Batts shouldered open the door, they found Lord Dudley on the floor behind his desk. Dead—a bullet hole in his head. Clutched in his right hand was a fireplace poker. Marie noticed the open window and the brisk breeze. Captain Batts noticed the open desk drawer and the revolver lying in the bottom of it. But it was Lady Dudley who noticed the empty velvet pouch.

Exactly one month later, Lord Dudley's accused killer comes to trial. "Kat Burghar, the Deadly Cat Burglar," had been on every front page in Britain. You've seen her picture a hundred times. But sitting here in the defendant's box in His Majesty's court, she is even more attractive than you imagined. The Prosecution states its case.

PROSECUTION: Miss Katrina Burghar is a daring woman with a lust for precious gems. She was determined to get her hands on the Asprey diamonds and saw the dumbwaiter as the perfect means. This pulley-operated mechanism was used to lift food and plates from the basement kitchen to the dining room. It also opened on the second-floor master suite and on the guest bedroom above that. By squeezing her petite frame into this mini-elevator and pulling the ropes, Miss Burghar managed to lift herself unseen from the dining room to her victim's bedroom, where she killed her host, stole the diamonds, then retraced her route. If the family butler had not been in the dining room just as Miss

Burghar emerged from the dumbwaiter, she might never have been caught.

Trial Witnesses & Evidence

This crime can be solved with 3 clues.

Defense Witness, Katrina Burghar

KATRINA BURGHAR: I did it as a lark— to see if I could really fit in and do it. If I got stuck, I figured I could always call out and either Lord Dudley or Captain Batts would hear me. There was no way I could get into their rooms by myself. The dumbwaiter door can only be opened from the outside.

DEFENSE: Please describe your experience.

KATRINA BURGHAR: I was in the dining room. Alone. I heard an odd noise, like something falling down the chute. When I first opened the dumbwaiter, the box was on the third floor, so I had to pull it down. Then I squeezed myself in and began to pull up. I only managed to move a few feet and then . . . The first gunshot was terribly frightening. Right afterwards I heard some mumbling, like a man talking to himself. Then came the second shot and I lowered myself down. The butler was there when I came out.

PROSECUTION CROSS-EXAMINATION: Do you really expect us to believe you did this just as a lark?

KATRINA BURGHAR: It's the truth.

PROSECUTION: And what were you wearing for this rather athletic lark of yours?

KATRINA BURGHAR: Umm. I had changed into a black, sleeveless silk dress.

Prosecution Witness, Officer on the Scene

OFFICER: We assume it was the first shot that missed, since the witnesses described a heavy thud after the second. For the longest time we couldn't locate that first bullet. It was in the ceiling, clear across the room from the desk where the body was found. The desk's bottom right drawer was open about a quarter of the way. There were fresh scratches in the wood of the drawer's inside edge. These scratches match tiny slivers of wood on the sides of the revolver handle. The window was open, but there was no sign of an intruder. The door to the dumbwaiter was closed.

PROSECUTION: Can the dumbwaiter be opened from the inside?

OFFICER: No. But you can close it from the inside. The deceased could have opened it. As she left, Miss Burghar could have closed it.

PROSECUTION: Did you find Miss Burghar's prints in the room?

OFFICER: No. But we did find a pair of men's gloves beside the body. Traces of gun oil were on them.

Defense Cross-Examination, Officer on the Scene

DEFENSE: What did you find when you searched Miss Burghar's possessions?

OFFICER: Nothing. I mean we found no trace of the diamonds, neither on her person nor anywhere in the mansion or the garden.

DEFENSE: Did you find anything at all?

OFFICER: Yes. We found paste copies of the Asprey diamonds. Good imitations, too. They were in the bottom of the dumbwaiter chute.

DEFENSE: What made you search the dumbwaiter chute?

OFFICER: When we questioned Miss Burghar, she mentioned hearing something go down the chute.

DEFENSE: So, if she had not mentioned that noise, you might not have examined the chute?

OFFICER: We might have, eventually.

Prosecution Exhibit A, Revolver

The Prosecution introduces the murder weapon into evidence. A Scotland Yard firearms expert describes it as an American-made revolver, known to have been part of the deceased's gun collection, which he usually kept under lock and key in a downstairs display case.

FIREARMS EXPERT: There were no prints on the revolver, but we did find several fresh scratches on the trigger. Horizontal scratches, probably made by a hard metal object.

Coroner's Evidence

CORONER: He was killed by a single gunshot. The bullet entered the right jaw at a steep upward trajectory and lodged itself in the upper left hemisphere of the cerebrum. There was no evidence of a struggle.

DEFENSE CROSS-EXAMINATION: Assuming that the first shot missed its target, wouldn't you have expected to find evidence of a struggle?

CORONER: Perhaps.

DEFENSE: Lord Dudley was in debt, yet he continued to maintain a generous life-insurance policy. Has Scotland Yard ruled out suicide?

CORONER: The evidence does not seem to support this possibility. The revolver was fired from 6 feet away and was found inside the drawer, several feet from the body. Also, at the time of his death, Lord Dudley had his gun hand occupied. He was holding a poker.

Will-o'-the-Wisp

"A GUNSHOT," REGGIE LONG yelled into the receiver. "And a split-second after that I heard a shout, a man's shout." He was still gazing out his living room window at the front of the house next door. "No one's come or gone. It's 412 Maple Street. Hurry."

The police dispatcher said a patrol car would be there within minutes, warning him not to leave his house. But Reggie's curiosity would not be denied. He slipped on his coat, grabbed a set of keys from a peg, and trudged out into a foot-deep carpet of newly fallen snow. Arthur, the neighbor from the other side of 412 Maple, was already standing at Gus's front door. "Arthur? Is anyone answering? I have a house key Gus gave me."

Arthur Ames pounded a fist on the door. "Gus?" he yelled, then tried the knob. "It's locked. Gus?" He waited several seconds, coatless and shivering. "OK. Give me the key."

The entry hall was dark as the neighbors stepped into the elegant house that separated their own residences. They didn't have to wander far to find the body. Gus Goode was lying in the doorway to his downstairs study, a pool of blood surrounding his head. Five feet away lay a .38 revolver. "Is anyone there?" a voice wailed from the second floor. "Something woke me. It sounded like . . . Is Gus all right? Gus?"

The neighbors knew the voice—Lydia, Gus's ailing, bedridden wife. Before either could answer her or approach the corpse, the blare of a siren became audible, growing louder with each passing second.

Right off, the police noticed footprints. The snow had stopped a half-hour earlier and the white lawn of 412 was dotted with two clearly marked trails, one set leading from Reggie's house, the other from Arthur's, both trails converging on 412's doorstep. As expected, they found their suspect still inside. Joey Goode was Gus and Lydia's nephew, a deaf-mute who had been living with the elderly couple for the past year. When the police searched the third floor, they found Joey in his room watching the last of his morning shows on a soundless TV, seemingly unaware of the murder that had taken place just two floors below.

The alleged motive was found clenched in the victim's fist. Arthur, the family lawyer as well as neighbor, recognized the scrap of torn paper. "It's a corner of Gus's new will. He signed it last night. See here? The date. And part of the signatures of the witnesses, Reggie and me. I know it's not usual for a lawyer to witness a client's will. But Gus was insistent on getting it done right away. Lydia couldn't sign because she inherits."

Naturally, the police wanted to see a copy of the will. Arthur led the way to his own house. And that's where they encountered the day's second crime. "It's gone," Arthur said as he fumbled through his papers. "The only other copy of Gus's new will is gone. I put it in this file just last night."

No trace of either copy was ever found—not a shred, ash, or any other remnant—which made Gus's old will once again valid. The district attorney begins his opening argument.

PROSECUTION: Joey Goode had motive. He inherited under the old will, but not under the new. He was the only one with opportunity. No footprints other than the witnesses' were found in the snow. Also, the front door. It's not equipped with an automatic lock, which means that someone leaving the house could not simply pull the door locked behind him. He would have had to use a key. And yet the witnesses tell us the door was locked, another indication of an inside job.

It seems pretty conclusive. Joey had been the only physically capable person in a house cut off by a blanket of untrampled snow. But, as you view the evidence, something doesn't seem quite right.

Trial Witnesses & Evidence

This crime can be solved with 1 clue.

Prosecution Witness, Reggie Long

PROSECUTION: How long after the shot did it take you to look out the window to the victim's door?

REGGIE LONG: No time at all. I was right by the window.

PROSECUTION: And after that, how long was the door out of your sight?

REGGIE LONG: Ten seconds maximum. Just long enough to grab my coat and keys and head out the door.

PROSECUTION: And while you were watching, no one left the Goode house?

REGGIE LONG: No one.

PROSECUTION: Now, Mr. Long, about the will. You acted as a witness on the night before the murder.

REGGIE LONG: Correct. Arthur called me up and asked me to come over. It was quite late. He explained that I was witnessing Gus's signature. Gus was in a mean mood, mean but very aware of what he was doing. It just took a minute.

Prosecution Witness, Arthur Ames

ARTHUR AMES: Just like Reggie, I heard the gunshot and the shout. I had an instant feeling it might be Gus. Without thinking, I rushed right out the door, straight into the snow. It wasn't easy going. Some of the drifts were 2 feet high. I got to Gus's door about the same time Reggie came out. I saw absolutely no one but Reggie outside, not until the police showed up a minute or so later.

PROSECUTION: Do you remember seeing any footprints at all, other than your own?

ARTHUR AMES: There were no other prints.

Defense Witness, Investigating Officer

DEFENSE: Did you find any trace of an intruder?

INVESTIGATING OFFICER: We're not sure. You see, in the hall closet we found four coats—three large males and a medium female. Also, three pairs of snow boots, two male and a female, and a pair of rubbers. The rubbers and one of the male coats were wet, as was the floor in front of the closet. We asked Mrs. Goode to identify the coats, and she could not be sure which ones belonged to her husband and nephew. If one of the men owned two coats and a pair of rubbers, then no, there was no intruder. On the other hand, an intruder could have arrived just as it started snowing, hung up his coat, killed Goode, then somehow got away, leaving his coat and rubbers behind. Theoretically.

PROSECUTION CROSS-EXAMINATION: How many keys exist to the front door?

INVESTIGATING OFFICER: Three. Mrs. Goode is positive about that. We've accounted for all three. One was in Joey Goode's pocket, one on the deceased's key chain, and one in Mr. Long's possession, the one used to unlock the door.

PROSECUTION: And was there any way of locking that door without a key?

INVESTIGATING OFFICER: No.

Prosecution Witness, Medical Examiner

MEDICAL EXAMINER: Death was administered by a single shot from an unregistered .38 revolver. The bullet pierced the forehead, passing through both the frontal lobe and postcentral gyrus and lodging in the parietal lobe. I would have to say that death was nearly instantaneous.

Prosecution Exhibit C, Old Will

The Prosecution introduces the contents of Gus Goode's old will. In the absence of any later document, this testament is legally binding. In this will, Gus leaves the bulk of his estate to his wife and nephew, evenly divided between them, with a smaller inheritance going to his lawyer and childhood friend, Arthur Ames. Small bequests are also allocated to other friends and distant relatives.

A Family Feud

Dr. PHILIP BROMLEY was overseeing the admission of his patient to Mt. Cedar Hospital. "It's a broken tibia," he told the administrator as he showed her the X rays. "I put Kurt McCoy in an inflatable leg cast. He can't walk on it. He'll need at least a day's rest and observation. To be honest, the fracture was a result of a fight between Mr. McCoy and his cousin. Until things cool down between the McCoys, I just think it better for Kurt to stay here."

Kurt and Emil McCoy had jointly inherited the family garment business, but their relationship soon deteriorated. The latest incident was a slugfest during which Emil swore that he would kill Kurt and then proceeded to smash his lower left leg with a baseball bat. Kurt needed some place safe to stay while he recovered from the trauma and worked out a lawsuit against his cousin. Hence, Mt. Cedar.

Dr. Bromley wheeled Kurt into his private room and made sure the window was latched. It was 8 P.M. The hospital ordered a security guard to monitor the hall and made a note on Kurt's chart not to disturb him until morning.

At around 2 A.M. a nurse ignored that note and poked her head into room 507. She saw no trace of her patient but did notice an open window. A deflated leg cast on the sill prompted her to peer out the window. Nothing was on the fire escape. But below it, in the deserted alley, lay the body of Kurt McCoy face down on a pile of garbage bags.

The police initially assumed that Kurt had removed his cast and was trying to maneuver his way down the fire escape when he lost his balance. But that was before they saw the bullet hole. A .38 slug had penetrated the victim's chest and proved to be the cause of death.

Emil was interviewed the next day at McCoy Fashion's office and warehouse in an industrial section of town. Emil showed no grief at the news. "Well, at least he won't be suing me." When asked for his whereabouts between 9 P.M. and midnight, Emil had his answer ready. "I was here in the office.

We were having trouble with our Hong Kong suppliers. I was calling them or they were calling me all night long. I picked up my car at about 1 A.M. Feel free to check with the phone company and the garage man."

When the grand jury convenes two weeks later, it's not Emil who stands accused of killing Kurt McCoy. It's the doctor.

PROSECUTION: The Prosecution will point out the discrepancies in Dr. Bromley's story. Kurt McCoy died between 9 and midnight. According to the guard in the hall, Dr. Bromley visited Mr. McCoy at 12:30, at least half an hour after he'd been dead, and made this notation on his chart: "12:30. Resting peacefully." And yet at that time, McCoy was already dead. The doctor has no explanation for this except to say that the coroner must be wrong. (*The district attorney counts off on his fingers.*) The door was guarded, the window locked. The victim feared for his life and trusted only Dr. George Bromley. Only Dr. Bromley had access. And he lied about Mr. McCoy being alive at 12:30.

DEFENSE: The Prosecution has no evidence. My client had no motive. He owns no gun, nor was any gun found among his possessions. The guard, who'd been outside the room all during Dr. Bromley's 12:30 visit, heard no sound. No gunshots, no struggle. Nothing. This grand jury should never have been called.

Your job as a grand jury is not to judge the guilt or innocence of Dr. Bromley but to determine whether or not there is enough evidence to hold him for trial. Despite this simple directive, you cannot help looking at the larger picture. How exactly did Kurt McCoy die and who killed him?

Trial Witnesses & Evidence

This crime can be solved with 2 clues.

Prosecution Witness, Officer on the Scene

PATROLMAN ENGELS: I was the first to arrive in the alley at 2:14 A.M. The body of the victim, Kurt McCoy, was face down on some garbage bags. The body was cool to the touch and totally naked except for a wristband identifying the patient and his room number. An hour or so later, when the coroner allowed the body to be moved, I noticed that there was little blood on the bags, less than I'd imagine given the nature of the wound. We also found no blood in Mr. McCoy's room. Underneath the body were several broken pieces of glass, probably from a drinking glass.

Coroner's Report

The coroner reads from his report and states that the time of death was definitely between 9 P.M. and midnight.

CORONER: Death was caused by a single gunshot wound to the chest, severing the right coronary artery and causing the victim to quickly bleed to death. Other damage to the body included a severely fractured fibula [bone] in the lower left leg. The tibia [bone] was bruised but not broken.

Prosecution Witness, Telephone Technician

In an attempt to eliminate Emil McCoy, the only other principal suspect, the Prosecution calls Bruce Turner, a telephone company technician. Mr. Turner, who reviewed records from the night of the murder, states that Emil McCoy had definitely been speaking on his office instrument.

BRUCE TURNER: No cellular phones had been used to transmit or receive any of the calls. Neither had any special services, such as call-forwarding, been used to mask the destination of an incoming call. The longest time elapsing between calls was approximately 20 minutes.

PROSECUTION: And, with no traffic, the McCoy office and warehouse are approximately 15 minutes away from Mt. Cedar Hospital.

Defense Witness, Mrs. Barbara Connor (Room 407)

DEFENSE: Mrs. Connor, you were a patient in the room directly below Mr. McCoy's. Did you see or hear anything the night of the murder that might be of interest to this court?

BARBARA CONNOR: I suppose. You see, I woke up late. It was a warm night and my window was open. Anyway, I reached out for some water on the nightstand. I was kind of groggy, and when I stuck out my hand I brushed my glass of water out the window. That woke me up. I got up and looked out to see if it had hit anybody.

DEFENSE: And what did you see?

BARBARA CONNOR: Well, right below my window was this alley. There were some garbage bags there. My glass landed on top of a bag and had broken into a couple of pieces. There was no body in the alley, just the bags.

DEFENSE: And when did this take place?

BARBARA CONNOR: I checked my clock just before going back to sleep. It was exactly 12:12.

The Prosecution seems eager to cross-examine the witness, but since this is only a grand jury, it does not have the opportunity.

Prosecution Witness, Nurse on Duty

The nurse who entered Kurt McCoy's room testifies that she looked out the window and discovered the body at 2 A.M. She was impressed by the fact that the victim was naked, and this led her to check around. She found Kurt McCoy's hospital clothes neatly piled on a chair. Looking into the closet of his hospital room, she found that Mr. McCoy's street clothes were missing, as were his wallet and keys. His crutches were still propped against the wall where she had last seen them. A police witness confirms later that the victim's street clothing was never found.

PROSECUTION: Did anything unusual happen that evening, before you discovered the body?

NIGHT NURSE: Yes. I was on the second floor at about 1:30, taking a break, when I noticed a man wandering around the halls. He seemed to be checking the room numbers on the doors. Before I could call out to him, he disappeared down a flight of stairs.

One Strike, You're Out

The prosecutor was doing her best to make the meek bantamweight look like a monster.

Prosecution: Glen Weaver's plan was diabolically simple. For weeks, the neighborhood of Regal Park had been plagued by burglaries. But Glen's wife, Dora, wasn't worried. A first-rate alarm system protected their home. Then, so very conveniently, on the morning of her murder, the alarm broke down. Dora stayed home from work that day waiting for a repairman who never showed up, a repairman that her husband had never called. And with good reason. For if the alarm had been fixed, Glen Weaver would never have been able to bludgeon his wife to death and try to blame it on a nonexistent burglar.

The murder had been discovered by Jimmy and Johnny Hall. At 5:30 p.m., the teenage brothers had just started batting baseballs in the park behind the Weaver home. Jimmy hit a long one and, as bad luck would have it, they heard the shattering of glass. Being honest boys, Jimmy and Johnny began walking toward the row of houses. A man in the house next door had also heard the crash. He came out onto his patio and looked around. "Looks like you boys are going to have to deal with Dora Weaver," he said, pointing to the kitchen door in the Weaver house. There was a hole in the lower left of the door's window. The man joined the boys and was about to knock on the door when he happened to glance through the window. "Good heavens!" Dora Weaver was lying in the middle of the kitchen, her head surrounded by a pool of blood.

Both the neighbor and the boys stared at the body, then glanced up. Glen Weaver was standing in the dining-room doorway, a bloody rolling pin clutched in his hand. He seemed dazed and shocked. On seeing the three faces in the window, Glen dropped the weapon and hurried away. "Where's my ball?" Jimmy asked as he scanned the kitchen floor. His brother told him to shut up.

PROSECUTION: The Defense is going to tell you that Glen Weaver had just arrived home from work, that he had just poured himself a scotch in the living room, that he heard the crash of glass and that when he walked into the kitchen, his wife's body was already there. They're going to tell you that a stunned Mr. Weaver picked up the rolling pin, not realizing that it was the murder weapon.

Well, our response is simple. We will show that the Weaver home had been sealed, every door and window locked from the inside. Even if Mrs. Weaver had admitted her killer, she couldn't very well have bolted the door after he left. Plus, there was no sign of forced entry. A witness, Mrs. Weaver's aunt, was in the house, in her wheelchair by a second-floor window. She will testify that no one even approached the front door until Glen Weaver unlocked it at 5:25 P.M.

The evidence is simple and straightforward. Had it not been for the baseball, Glen Weaver would have had all the time he needed to wipe his prints off the rolling pin, force a door or window and create the charade of a brutal murder occurring during a robbery attempt. Thank heavens for baseball! It's baseball that will help us convict a cold-blooded killer.

The Defense waives its opening statement and you feel sorry for little Mr. Weaver. He certainly doesn't look cold-blooded. But if he didn't kill his wife, who did?

Trial Witnesses & Evidence

This crime can be solved with 2 clues.

Prosecution Witness, Dora's Aunt
PROSECUTION: Ms. Burden, did you see Mr. Weaver come home?

DORA'S AUNT: Yes. I was sitting by my window. Glen came home about 5:25 in the evening.

PROSECUTION: Did you hear any noises from downstairs? The attack on your niece? The sound of breaking glass?

DORA'S AUNT: No. I'd turned my hearing aid off.

PROSECUTION: Was Mr. Weaver aware that you often turned off your hearing aid?

DORA'S AUNT: Yes. He was the one who suggested it. I hate street noise.

PROSECUTION: So, Glen Weaver knew you would not be able to hear when he attacked his wife?

DEFENSE: Objection.

JUDGE: Objection sustained.

DEFENSE CROSS-EXAMINATION: How do you manage to get up and down the stairs?

DORA'S AUNT: The staircase is equipped with an electric riding chair. There's a wheelchair at the bottom that I can lift myself into. It takes effort, but I can manage.

DEFENSE: So, you can move between floors if you really have a need to?

DORA'S AUNT: Yes.

Prosecution Witness, Burglar Alarm Repairman

REPAIRMAN: According to our records, we never received a call from Mr. Weaver about a breakdown. We've been getting a lot of work lately on account of the burglaries in the area.

PROSECUTION: Did you install the Weaver system?

REPAIRMAN: Yeah, about 3 months ago. It was a silent alarm that automatically rang the police. Mrs. Weaver didn't want any obvious signs that the house was protected. We told her the more obvious the alarm, the more it would discourage burglars. But she thought alarm strips and wires were ugly.

PROSECUTION: Did you inspect the alarm system after the murder?

REPAIRMAN: Yes. Some wires had jiggled loose in the connection box. A 2-minute repair job.

Prosecution Witness, Robert Jenkins (Neighbor)

The witness describes events leading up to his discovery of the body, including Glen Weaver's appearance and actions when he saw him in the kitchen. On cross-examination, Jenkins admits that Weaver's behavior could also be in keeping with his story that the accused was stunned and picked up the bloody rolling pin by accident.

DEFENSE: Is it true, Mr. Jenkins, that on the evening of the murder you rushed out to a building supply store and insisted that they open up for you so that you could buy a new kitchen door?

ROBERT JENKINS: Yes. I bought a reinforced steel door without a window.

DEFENSE: And why did you do that?

ROBERT JENKINS: My old door was pretty flimsy, and I wanted protection, especially after what happened to Dora.

DEFENSE: So, despite what you saw, you thought Mrs. Weaver had been attacked by a burglar and not by Mr. Weaver. That's what your actions seem to indicate.

ROBERT JENKINS: I guess so.

Defense Witness, Officer on the Scene

OFFICER: Mr. Glen Weaver reported the crime at 5:34 P.M. He said he had just come home. He'd heard glass breaking but could not tell where it came from. He went back into the kitchen and that's when he found his wife. At 5:35 we received a similar call from Mr. Robert Jenkins next door. Me and my partner arrived at 5:40. Jimmy and Johnny Hall were on the front lawn. Mr. Weaver was upstairs with the victim's aunt. He came down to let us in.

The first thing I saw when I entered the kitchen was Dora Weaver lying on her back. There was a bloody concussion on her left temple, indicating she had been attacked from the front. The rolling pin was by the dining-room door. There were signs of a struggle: torn clothing, things knocked off counters. There were also glass fragments on the floor by the back door. Oh, and the baseball, beside the body about a foot away.

DEFENSE: In your opinion, were there any signs of a burglary?

OFFICER: No obvious signs. No.

Prosecution Witness, Dora Weaver's Sister

KAREN LANGFORD: I loved Dora, but she was always a bit of a shrew. Poor henpecked Glen put up with an awful lot. It's no wonder he finally snapped.

DEFENSE CROSS-EXAMINATION: How long were they married?

KAREN LANGFORD: Fifteen years.

DEFENSE: If things were so bad, why didn't they get a divorce?

KAREN LANGFORD: Dora talked about divorce. But Glen always wound up apologizing for things that were Dora's fault, and somehow they stayed together.

DEFENSE: Were there any reasons that he shouldn't have divorced her? Money? Children?

KAREN LANGFORD: No.

DEFENSE: So, maybe the reason they stayed together was because he loved her.

KAREN LANGFORD: Maybe.

Jury Deliberations

Stories are arranged alphabetically.

"Death & the Single Girl" Deliberations

The first thing the jury examines is the torn photo. This Christmas photo was obviously taken before Ginger moved to town last April. You and other jury members theorize that it was a picture of Ginger and her *previous* boyfriend and that Ginger herself tore off the half she no longer wanted. This leads to another theory, that it was Ginger's previous boyfriend and not Todd who was scheduled to meet her on the night of the murder.

You shift focus to Paul Gruber and the discrepancies in his story. For instance, Paul initially described Ginger's apartment as "deadly quiet." Yet, as he was leaving, Paul said he could hear running water and used this excuse to turn off the bathroom faucets.

Most jury members have no idea of what part the wet towels played, but the fact that they were found in the garbage with the gloves links them to the murder. Their location, stuck between Paul's floor and Ginger's, further implicates Paul. Or possibly Archie.

Going in Paul's favor is the fact that Ginger told the doorman she was expecting a guest. Since Paul and Archie lived in the building, they would not have to be admitted. And had the doorman really been on duty all evening or not? Another discrepancy.

"A Family Feud" Deliberations

The broken glass under the body lends credence to the testimony of the patient in room 407. If there had been a body in the alley at 12:12 P.M., then the glass would have been found on top of it, not underneath. The lack of blood in the room and the minimal amount in the alley supports the same conclusion. Kurt McCoy was killed elsewhere and moved after death.

Since the guard stated emphatically that no one but Dr. Bromley had entered the room, whoever else entered or left the room must have done so through the window, which had been latched from the inside.

Had Kurt really been resting comfortably at 12:30 as Dr. Bromley said? If so, then the coroner was wrong about the time of death. In addition, which leg bone had been broken? The fibula, according to the coroner's report, or the tibia, according to Dr. Bromley's X ray? Dr. Bromley may not be the killer, but he certainly seems to be hiding something.

Other facts seem equally mysterious. Why was the body naked? Why were the victim's street clothes, wallet, and keys missing? And who was that man wandering around the second floor of the hospital around 1:30 the night of the murder?

"The Haunted House Murder" Deliberations

In the jury room you spend a few hours reviewing physical evidence. The animal blood seems particularly problematic.

Just as confusing is the second knife, which was supposedly carried by the figure Anne saw in the hall. Since this knife was found nearby and had been in contact with the same type of animal blood, this broken weapon appears to be connected to the crime. A fellow juror suggests Lilly had stumbled onto some kind of ritualistic ceremony involving animal sacrifice.

While the crime scene evidence shows that the defendant

had been in the room, it does not connect Billy Willis directly to the crime. In fact, the lack of bloody fingerprints on the grisly scene is a point in his favor. The defendant's alibi also seems plausible. If a drunk buys alcohol at 11 P.M., chances are good that he will begin drinking right away. By midnight, Willis could well have been much too drunk to be capable of committing such a strenuous act.

A female juror points out a discrepancy between the way the police described the knife's position and the way the Prosecution described it in her opening statement. You review the transcripts but draw no conclusions about what this means.

"The Hot Designer" Deliberations

The first thing you and fellow jurors focus on is the cause of death. Despite the evidence of the beach umbrella, several jurors doubt that a simple house fire could be intense enough to inflict that kind of damage to the body. Fried nerves? That seems very hot, indeed. And why was there no evidence of smoke inhalation?

A fellow juror points out the absurdity of making a cellphone call from a house filled with regular phones. But then, fashion people are a little absurd to start with. And the Defense's obsession with the cellular phone mystifies you. Even if the charred telephone belonged to someone else, Ms. Vanushka had still made a call from her own phone to her secretary from 7:53 to 8:05 P.M. This has been documented by the secretary herself. To doubt this is to conclude that the secretary is lying about who called her. Why would she do that?

"The Lady in the Dumbwaiter" Deliberations

The fact that Katrina Burghar mentioned the sound of the fake diamonds being dropped down the chute points to her innocence. But her story about playing with the dumbwaiter just for a lark is highly suspect, given her black silk dress. A much more likely story is that she had an assignation with someone on the second or third floor and saw the dumbwaiter as a way of secretly gaining access.

Other jurors are just as confused as you are by the details. For instance, Lord Dudley saw an intruder in the garden and his bedroom window was open on a chilly night. Yet no trace of an intruder was found. In addition, the upward angle of the two shots would have put Dudley and his killer in very odd positions. The multiple scratches on the drawer, gun handle, and trigger also have to be explained somehow.

But the most confusing aspect of the crime concerns the Asprey Whites. Why had someone constructed paste forgeries and then thrown those forgeries down the chute? And what about the real Asprey Whites? What ever happened to them?

"No Brake for the Wearys" Deliberations

Female jury members agree that the prenuptial agreement was unfair. A young, desirable woman married to an extremely wealthy elderly man deserved more than $200,000 in a divorce settlement.

Male jury members, however, concentrate on the oil change. What about the lack of used oil, oily rags, and oilcans? This seems to incriminate Adam. The fresh oil stain on the floor, however, does seem to support his story.

When discussing cars, a jury member poses an interesting question: How could Adam have known that the Wearys would be using only one car? Since the couple had separate plans for the rest of the day, it seems logical that they would have used both cars.

You and other jury members focus on the condition of Pauline's body. What is the significance of the severe contusion that occurred prior to death, probably suffered on the path from the house to the garage? The state of her dress and the presence of blood on the path also point to this conclusion. Pauline evidently had been injured prior to getting in the car.

The receipt found in the Cadillac seems to give Adam a viable alibi. But if Adam did not tamper with the car, who did?

What really happened on the afternoon of May 15? Is Adam Weary guilty or not? Your jury has been arguing for two days.

"One Strike, You're Out" Deliberations

As you confer, you agree that the most disturbing aspect of this case is the apparent lack of motive. Glen Weaver seemed to have no reason, financial or otherwise, to murder his wife of 15 years. But if Glen didn't kill her, then who did? And why? The only other person in the locked house was Dora's aunt. The aunt could move between floors by herself. But remember, there was a struggle. The aunt would probably not be the winner in any fight with her niece.

One juror nominates the alarm-system repairman. What if he were the neighborhood burglar? He could have let himself into the house, perhaps with the key he had made on his previous visit. Who would make a better burglar than a security specialist? And it would also increase demand for his legitimate business. A nice theory, but there seems little evidence to support it.

Another juror suspects that Mr. Jenkins knows more than he's telling. Why was he so desperate to replace the back door of his house? Was he afraid of something? Or someone?

You, personally, wonder about the baseball. Why didn't Jimmy Hall see it when he looked around the kitchen floor?

"Our Man in the Field" Deliberations

The Prosecution has established that Okan was the unmasked robber, you and other jury members agree. Okan had been killed by the guard and was being dragged across the field by the accused. The dragging, however, presents problems. You need to consider that the bloody path leads to the center of the field, well beyond the spot where Heath was caught with the body. Also, both the shovel and car were clean of the deceased's blood, clothing fibers, and hair. Heath, you conclude, must have been dragging the body *to* his car, and not from it.

Although the Defense may not realize it, Wally Heath's laundry helps confirm his alibi. The dirty water indicates that Wally Heath started the cycle after 8:55. Most wash cycles are 30 to 40 minutes long. Since the bank alarm went off at 9:08 and the bank was 7 miles from the defendant's house, he could not have both robbed the bank and been at home to put the laundry in the washer.

The only really incriminating piece of evidence, which had shocked Heath's attorney, was the discovery of human blood in the laundry room, in the kitchen, and outside the back door.

"Trial of the Black Widow" Deliberations

You wonder, with other jury members, how you could poison someone at a garden party. Could it have been a random act of buffet terrorism? Or had the poison been intended for someone else? You quickly put these thoughts aside. That's not your job. You're here to evaluate the innocence or guilt of one person, Anabel Lee Ricolah. The only hard evidence in this case is the trace of cyanide found in the plastic storage bag and on the grass.

JUROR: Can we trust Emma Peters as a witness? If we can, then we know that Anabel had contact with at least two storage bags, the one used to hold the drink garnishes and the one found in the electric ice cooler.

SECOND JUROR: That doesn't get us anywhere. Cyanide is a fast poison. There was no garnish in Victor's drink and he had been sipping it for a half-hour.

THIRD JUROR: The poison was in liquid form. It would have been hard to plant on a dry food like a potato chip. Hard but not impossible.

You decide to ask for the videotape from the bailiff and watch it again, hoping it will provide some inspiration. Anabel did buy liquid cyanide, and she certainly has a history of different names and dead husbands. But does that prove she's a killer?

"The Vanishing Verrocchio" Deliberations

When the case came to trial, the statue was still missing. You and a few other jury members feel uneasy about convicting anyone until after the Verrocchio sculpture is recovered. Also, several nagging questions cast doubt on Father Damien's guilt. Why, for instance, would he disguise himself with a hood and wear his own robe? And why would he throw his own robe over the wall rather than simply wearing it back to the manor house? And what about the Chinese pot? Why would Father Damien take a Chinese pot and put it out on the lawn? Why would anybody?

Other nagging questions focus attention on Edgar Chipping, the dead guard. Although he pointed in the defendant's direction, Edgar never directly accused Father Damien. And then there were his last words: "Priest stole. Here. Understand." Was he able to see the face inside the concealing hood? And what did he want them to understand?

"Will-o'-the-Wisp" Deliberations

You enter the jury room mulling over mounds of questions and inconsistencies. For starters, who shouted a split second after the murder? Since the victim was killed instantly, it couldn't have been he. The killer perhaps? An eyewitness? It certainly wasn't the deaf-mute defendant, Joey Goode.

Another juror points out a discrepancy between Arthur Ames's testimony and Reggie Long's. You didn't notice the discrepancy until she outlined it. But you still don't understand what it means.

And what about the disappearing wills? No trace of what would have been a multipage document was found anywhere in the snowbound house. Next door, at Arthur Ames's house, the lawyer and police also found nothing.

The final mystery is the lack of footprints in the snow. How would a killer or thief get into the Goode house on a snowy morning?

"A Witless Eyewitness?" Deliberations

You and other jury members combine the forensic evidence with the testimony of the two witnesses in the bar and agree with the Defense. The alley was the scene of the crime, and the time, 5:40 P.M.

Since there is no evidence indicating that Busby and the bartender are in collusion, you also conclude that both are innocent. Nevertheless, Busby's behavior seems noteworthy. He was in an unexpectedly good mood, and despite financial straits he ordered an expensive scotch. Several jurors want to connect this to the defendant's withdrawal of $10,000 from his bank.

The large amount of nitrate on Wade's hand proves that he had fired a weapon, while the trace of nitrate on the deceased's hand and in his pocket indicate that he had handled a fired gun, perhaps carrying it in his pocket. The distance of 8 feet between the gun and the victim goes against the theory of self-defense.

Despite all this, Alice Gabriel's testimony is hard to dismiss. The gunpowder smell mentioned by the police supports her story. She also seems to have no reason to lie. Perhaps she simply misinterpreted what she saw.

Verdicts

Stories are arranged alphabetically.

"Death & the Single Girl" Verdict

Since there is not enough evidence to convict, you and the jury quickly find Todd Iona *not guilty*.

You, however, have an interesting idea about wet towels and running water and you report it to the district attorney. A week later, the local papers announce the arrest of Archie Gill.

Following your lead, the police discovered that Archie and Ginger had been seriously involved and that Ginger moved to town to get away from him. A few months later Archie followed and, unknown to Ginger, moved in directly below her. One day, he approached her in the park. Ginger was frightened but agreed to a meeting at her place. It was during this confrontation that Archie knifed his ex-sweetheart to death.

Only after Archie went downstairs to clean up did he notice the missing button. And then he recalled Ginger pulling at his shirt. Archie knew he had to return to the scene and account for the incriminating button before the police arrived. Paul had once mentioned having a key to Ginger's apartment. Somehow Archie had to get him to open her door. He didn't call the doorman because he wasn't sure what the building protocol was. He might not have been allowed to accompany the doorman inside.

Archie removed the cheap acoustic tile from the bathroom ceiling of his and Paul's apartment and placed three sopping wet towels on top of it. When Paul came home, the towels provided a realistic impression of a bathroom leak from the apartment upstairs.

It didn't matter whether Ginger's sink was overflowing or not. The leak could just as easily have come from another source. But, finding himself alone in the bathroom, Archie turned on the faucets and blocked the overflow drain. By the time Paul and Archie finished inspecting the body and Archie had played his pop-the-button charade, the flood had developed enough to be convincing.

"A Family Feud" Verdict

Even though you don't believe Dr. Philip Bromley is guilty of murder, you do believe he is involved somehow, and that's sufficient reason for you to *remand him to trial.*

When this verdict is announced, Dr. Bromley turns white and volunteers a confession.

DR. PHILIP BROMLEY: I know I could lose my license, even go to jail. Anyway, Kurt McCoy came to me after his fight. He was intending to sue his cousin for assault. When I told him his leg wasn't broken, he asked me if there was any way we could fake a broken leg. He would pay me half of whatever he won. So I dusted off some old X rays and had Kurt admitted. I had no idea he was planning anything more than a little fraud.

That night I happened to be at the hospital seeing another patient. I looked in on Kurt at 12:30 and found his room empty. I didn't know what to do; so, I pretended he was still there. Raising the alarm would have simply drawn attention to the fact that he could walk.

It seemed pretty simple. Kurt was using me. Shortly after I gave the "Do not disturb" order, he must have taken off his cast, climbed out the window, and found a way to get to Emil's office, maybe a cab. He caught Emil there and tried to kill him. Emil must have turned the tables and killed Kurt instead.

Seeing the wristband, Emil deduced that Kurt must have sneaked out. After 1 A.M., when the streets were deserted, Emil drove the corpse back in his own car. By wandering the halls, he figured out where room 507 was and planted the corpse beneath the window. If Kurt had been found wearing street clothes, then people might conclude he had left the hospital willingly. So, Emil stripped the body, then broke Kurt's leg for real. Funny. Kurt worked so hard to give himself an alibi and all he wound up doing was giving his killer an alibi.

"The Haunted House Murder" Verdict
You find Billy Willis *not guilty*.

Egged on by your verdict, the district attorney kept the case open and eventually amassed enough evidence to prosecute Anne Kincaid. After hours of questioning, the 17-year-old broke down and confessed. For years, Anne had been jealous of her sister. Lilly got everything: praise and attention and, most galling of all, a first-rate education that their parents had saved years for.

It was Lilly who had thought up the prank. They would lure their boyfriends into the old mansion and then scare them with a murder, just as in the movies. Anne instantly saw how this fake murder could be turned into a real one. Lilly and their parents would pay for their favoritism. And Anne would be the one to go to Princeton.

During their exploration, Lilly tiptoed away and set up the grisly scene, smearing herself with chicken blood and sticking the broken-off knife into her blouse. Anne made sure the boys didn't get too close to the "body," at the same time making sure that she got a sufficient amount of blood on herself.

The only thing Anne needed now was a few moments alone with her sister. As soon as she'd tricked the boys into running off, Anne produced a real knife and stabbed Lilly to death. The second scream had also come from Lilly, and this time she wasn't acting. In the 30 seconds it took the boys to run back upstairs, Anne had wiped off the fake knife and thrown it out the window.

The chicken blood helped set the police on the right track. But the clincher was the murder weapon's position. Both Mark and Larry described the handle-grip as facing down. The police photos, however, showed it facing up. Someone had obviously removed the knife and reversed it. Or stuck in a new knife, one with a blade.

"The Hot Designer" Verdict

You find Harve Grant *not guilty.*

In a note to the district attorney, you encourage his office to check the burned mansion for a large food freezer. The police find just such a freezer. Inside it they discover frozen hair strands matching the victim's. An interrogation of Ms. Vanushka's secretary produces a confession.

SECRETARY: All right. Vera died four days before the fire. We were on the beach together, Manny, Vera, and I, when a storm suddenly came up. As we were carrying our things back, a bolt of lightning struck her beach umbrella. Killed instantly. Just a few feet from the house. The servants were all on vacation. No one else had seen it happen, just Manny and me.

We were devastated. Her death had occurred at the worst possible time. VDNY was days away from its public offering. Manny and I both owned stock. If knowledge of Vera's death could only be postponed, we could sell our shares and be rich. So we invented Vera's summer cold and for the next three days fooled everyone into believing she was alive. The freezer kept the body from deteriorating.

It was Manny who engineered the fire. It would thaw her out and disguise the lightning damage. Even the fried beach umbrella would be accepted as a natural result of fire. Manny laid out the body, rigged the toaster oven, then took Vera's cellular phone, leaving his own phone on the scene.

That night Manny called me on Vera's phone. I pretended it was her. His house is in the same cell, and the phone company had no idea exactly where the call originated. He said this would establish that Vera was still alive. It was all meant to look like an accident. We never intended for Harve to get caught in the middle. I'm glad the jury found him not guilty.

"The Lady in the Dumbwaiter" Verdict

You find Katrina Burghar *not guilty.*

There is only one explanation for the paste diamonds hidden in the chute and the absence of real diamonds. The twelve of you agree on the solution but pledge never to reveal it to anyone. It would only hurt the Dudleys and destroy the upcoming marriage.

Right after the stock-market crash, when Lord Dudley was in desperate need of money, he secretly sold his wife's diamonds and had paste replicas made. Business continued to worsen, however. When his wife discovered their straits, she decided to finally make the sacrifice and sell the Asprey Whites, which she didn't realize he had sold. The only way out for Lord Dudley, it seemed, was suicide. The right kind of suicide would preserve his family's good opinion of him, cancel his debts, and secure a substantial life insurance payoff.

Lord Dudley pretended to see an intruder. Then he disposed of the fakes in the chute and opened his bedroom window, setting the stage for his "murder" and the "burglary." He donned a pair of gloves, took the revolver from his collection, and wedged it into the outer jaw of his bottom desk drawer. Removing the gloves, he then lined up his head with the muzzle and used the poker to press back the trigger. He succeeded on his second attempt. The recoil sent the gun falling down *inside* the open drawer.

Meanwhile, Katrina was hatching her own plot. She was infatuated with her best friend's fiancé and devised the idea of using the dumbwaiter to pull herself up to Captain Batts's room, unseen by family or servants. Your jury is undecided about Batts. Was he a party to her romantic plot, or was she simply planning to surprise him with a knock on the dumbwaiter door? You'll never know.

"No Brake for the Wearys" Verdict

You all agree on reasonable doubt. You find Adam Weary *not guilty.*

A month after the verdict, Adam sells the mansion. The movers discover a diary hidden under Pauline's mattress. In the private journal, the dead woman described her chilling plan to kill her husband and frame her stepson.

As soon as Pauline signed the despised prenuptial agreement, she formed a plot to kill off George and get her hands on all his millions. She planned to invite Adam over and ask him to change the oil, securing his fingerprints on the underchassis of George's Cadillac. Pauline herself would then dispose of the oil-change equipment and sabotage the brakes, wearing gloves in order to eliminate her prints. After George died in the crash, she would tell the police that she had originally planned to ride with him and that Adam had evidently schemed to kill them both.

With this information in hand, the authorities piece together a scenario. Shortly after Adam changed the oil, George took out the car to buy milk and cigarettes. An hour later, Pauline sabotaged the brakes. Then, at about 1:25 P.M., the couple left the house, walking to the garage and their separate cars. But on the path, Pauline accidentally slipped on the wet gravel and fell, knocking herself unconscious.

George was frantic with worry and managed, despite his age, to lift his wife into the Cadillac, intending to drive her to the nearest emergency room. The end result, of course, was that

Pauline not only succeeded in killing her husband and framing her stepson, but also managed to accidentally kill herself.

"One Strike, You're Out" Verdict

You find Glen Weaver *not guilty.*

Your curiosity about Jimmy Hall's baseball leads to an interesting theory. All twelve of you have a private conference with the district attorney. A search warrant produces a horde of stolen goods and a confession from Robert Jenkins, the neighbor.

ROBERT JENKINS: I'm the guy who's been robbing houses. As for the Weavers, I didn't mean to kill nobody. I figured Dora and Glen were still at work. The old lady would be upstairs with her hearing aid off and I'd have the downstairs to myself. I had no idea about the alarm. I'm glad it was off.

So I break in around 5 o'clock, smashing the glass in the door so I can reach in for the knob. I barely get inside when Dora barges in. Crazy woman. She sees the broken glass and my gloves and she attacks. I grab the rolling pin to defend myself and . . . Well, you know.

I don't take anything, I'm too scared. I walk out, then reach in through the hole and bolt the door. I go home to my own kitchen. And then a little while later this baseball comes flying through the glass in my door. I go outside and I see these boys coming with their bats. They're looking around for their ball. I leave my kitchen door open so they can't see the broken window, then point to the hole in the Weaver window. The rest is all luck, Glen being there just at the right time.

I send the boys out front to wait for the cops, then slip the baseball in beside Dora. The only problem left is *my* broken glass. In the dark you could barely see, but I had to replace it right away. You know how hard it is finding a building supply store open at that hour?

"Our Man in the Field" Verdict

The Prosecution has not proven its case. You find Wallace Heath *not guilty*.

Minutes after the jury foreman reads the verdict, a rookie patrolman, exploring the field behind Wally Heath's house, discovers a body in the abandoned well. It is found to be the remains of Amanda Heath, Wally's missing wife, who had been stabbed to death with a kitchen knife.

Faced with this discovery, Wally breaks down. Two weeks before he had been arrested dragging Okan's body, Wally had yet another explosive domestic quarrel, lost his temper, and killed his wife. He dumped the body into the well and invented the story about Amanda running off with a salesman. Since Amanda had no family and few friends nearby, everyone readily believed Wally's tale.

On the night of the robbery, Wally was in the laundry room when he happened to look out his window. By the light of the full moon, he could see a man drag a body into the field, dumping it only a few dozen yards from the well.

Wally went crazy with worry. The man's body was bound to be discovered. And when it was, the police would make a thorough search, finding Amanda in the process. Wally had no choice. He had to move the new body. If it were found anywhere else, the police would have no reason to scour this little field, and Amanda could rest in peace.

Unfortunately, the county workers saw him in the moonlight just as he began to drag the burglar's body to his car. It was, of course, preferable to be convicted of bank robbery than of murder. So, Wally said nothing to incriminate himself.

In his confession, Wally describes the bank robber's getaway car and the man he saw depositing the body in the field. Judd Okan's cousin is soon arrested on bank-robbery charges.

"Trial of the Black Widow" Verdict

You have no choice but to find Anabel Lee Long Lyons Leon Ricolah *not guilty*.

But during your two days of deliberation, you did manage to figure out how she *could* have arranged her husband's poisoning. A day before the party, Anabel could have worked up a special batch of ice cubes.

RECIPE: Fill ice tray one-third-full of water. While it freezes, boil a pan of marbles or some other small objects. Remove ice tray from freezer and place a hot marble in the center of each cube, just long enough to create a depression in the cube. Drain off melted water, then quickly fill the depression with liquid cyanide. Freeze the mixture, then fill the rest of ice tray with water and return to freezer. Keep in a cold, safe place until ready to use.

On the day of the party, Anabel could have filled a plastic bag with her poisoned cubes and stored it in the bottom of the electric cooler, beneath a hundred pounds of real ice. Having herself arranged the paltry supply of limes, she could have conveniently sent the bartender off for more, then mixed Victor's drink, adding her own special ice cubes. She would make sure to taste the drink in front of witnesses, then stay far away from Victor until the ice cubes melted and the cyanide was released. The dead grass could have been caused by Victor spilling the last of his poisoned drink.

Since Anabel wouldn't have had the chance to clean up after herself, she would have had to trust to fate. Remember, this was before anyone suspected murder. A person cleaning out the cooler would have simply tossed out the remaining ice and disposed of the bag.

"The Vanishing Verrocchio" Verdict

You find Father Damien *not guilty.*

As the bailiff read back Edgar's last words, a juror slightly hard-of-hearing heard something a little different. "Priest's hole. Maybe he said 'priest's *hole*,' not 'priest stole.' "

Yes, of course. Another jury member recalls that priests'

holes are hiding places found in many old English houses, concealed spaces where priests once hid from the authorities. Suddenly the case makes sense. The guilty party must be Lord George, the only member of the foursome who would know where a priest's hole could be found in Brighton Manor. You reconstruct the crime.

The earl of Brighton desperately wanted the bust but did not have the available cash. Rather than see it disappear into someone else's collection, he decided to steal it. Disguising himself with a hood and robe, Lord George entered the library, knocking out the guard. He then took the statue from its wooden stand and placed it in the priest's hole, directly under the parquet floor. That's what Edgar had meant by "understand": the priest's hole was *under*neath the *stand.*

The only problem remaining would have been to make it appear as if the statue had been removed from the estate. Lord George obviously knew about the videocamera and made sure that it recorded the image of a priest carrying out a weighted sack. The contents of the sack? The Chinese pot.

Once out on the grounds, Lord George removed the pot, and threw the sack, hood, and robe over the wall, hoping to implicate Father Damien. The guard's dying words made his effort nearly perfect.

The jury sends a note out to the judge and you receive confirmation within the hour. The St. Augustine bust was right where you said it would be, and that's all the proof you needed to find Damien not guilty.

"Will-o'-the-Wisp" Verdict

You find Joey Goode *not guilty.*

A glaring inconsistency guides you along the right path. It is illegal to witness a will in which you inherit. The fact that Arthur Ames signed the new will as a witness meant that *he* had been cut out, not Joey Goode. Suddenly, Arthur has a motive for killing Gus and destroying the new will. With this in mind, you construct the scenario.

On the night before the murder, Gus Goode wrote a new will, disinheriting his old friend and lawyer. The reason? You don't know.

Arthur was angered by Gus's behavior and visited his neighbor the next morning, just as it stopped snowing. Perhaps Arthur intended the meeting to be peaceful, although the unregistered gun in his pocket would indicate otherwise.

Gus and Arthur argued. Arthur brandished the weapon and it went off. The shout was Arthur's, delivered in shocked surprise at his own lethal action. After a minute of indecision, Arthur stuffed the will into his pocket and left, forgetting his overcoat and rubbers in the hall closet. Just as Arthur closed the door, Reggie Long popped out of his front door and naturally assumed Arthur had just arrived. The discrepancy between Reggie and Arthur's testimonies? Reggie said he turned away from his view of the house for only 10 seconds, hardly enough time for Arthur to leave his own house and trudge through the snow to his neighbor's.

Gus's front door was still unlocked. But when Reggie ran up and offered his key, Arthur was quick to take advantage, pretending to unlock an already unlocked door.

The only remaining problem was to make his own copy of the will disappear. Since Arthur was not a suspect, it was relatively easy for him to search through the wrong files and to dispose of the telltale document while the police looked elsewhere.

You aren't surprised when, a week later, Arthur Ames is arrested. After all, the police aren't stupid. They're just a little slower than you.

"A Witless Eyewitness?" Verdict

You and fellow jurors argue endlessly, trying to reconcile Alice Gabriel's story with the rest of the evidence. After three days of deliberation, you finally deliver your verdict, finding Wade Poe *guilty of first-degree murder.*

The key to the case was a passing comment by Wade's wife,

stating that he had been doing research on low-lifes and con artists. The mystery, you discover, hinges on an old con game played by Sonny and Busby on the naïve defendant.

The fight and "murder" that Alice witnessed from her window had actually been staged for Wade's benefit. Sonny loaded the silver .22 with blanks, then forced Wade to "kill" him in self-defense. When Busby walked into the apartment a few seconds later, Wade was desperate, prepared to do anything to avoid a murder charge. Busby said he would keep his mouth shut and dispose of Sonny's body for a payment of $10,000. Wade had no choice but to agree.

Wade rushed to his bank and quickly delivered the money to Busby. While Busby was celebrating with a drink at McGregor's, his partner Sonny was busy disposing of the evidence. But the two con artists had seriously underestimated their pigeon.

After paying off Busby, the writer began to have second thoughts. Had he been the victim of a con, like the cons Sonny and Busby always bragged about? Enraged by the thought, Wade retrieved his gun from his glove compartment and hid himself outside the house. When Sonny emerged, still very much alive, Wade followed him to McGregor's bar. There, in the alley, he confronted his tormentor and shot him to death, this time for real.

Index